ENVIRONMENTAL LAW

A Practical Handbook

ENVIRONMENTAL LAW

A Practical Handbook

John Garbutt,
Partner
Nicholson Graham & Jones, London

Chancery Law Publishing
London
1992

ENVIRONMENTAL LAW
A Practical Handbook

John Garbutt has been a solicitor for 28 years. He is a Partner and Head of the Planning and Environment Unit at City solicitors, Nicholson Graham & Jones; has been employed in local government and subsequently was chief executive of both the waste management and industrial minerals divisions at Blue Circles Industries. He also set up and ran their environmental affairs office. He is a member of the CBI Environmental Legislation Panel and has served on the Health and Safety Executive Advisory Committee on Major Hazards. He is a member of the UK Environmental Law Association speaking and writing extensively on environmental matters from a legal and managerial perspective.

Published in the United Kingdom by
Chancery Law Publishing Ltd
22 Eastcastle Street
London W1N 7PA

ISBN 1-85630-027-7

Photoset by Rowland Phototypesetting Ltd
Bury St Edmunds, Suffolk
Printed in Great Britain by Ipswich Book Co., Ipswich

For my father, one of that great body of solicitors whose dedication to their clients, great or small, is the strength of our profession.

Preface

Nicholson Graham & Jones is a leading City of London law firm founded in 1858. Its strengths are in company law, litigation, tax, pensions and property but in recent years it has developed a number of specialisms of which the Planning and Environment Unit is one of the more recent.

Even if the reader had been cut off from civilisation for some time he or she would not have failed to notice the extent to which, on a world scale, concern with the environment and the use of land and resources has become a major issue. To the lawyer, this manifests itself in an unprecedented range of new legislative and government initiatives which bear down mostly on the polluter but also on every individual. The impact of these changes at international level on our clients and others led us to establish the Planning and Environment Unit.

Given the great trend in the law to increase the size of practices and to develop large specialist groupings it is sometimes easy to forget that the strengths of the professions rest on a national pattern of small to medium sized practices whose partners and fee-earners need to have knowledge in many branches of the law. This book is aimed at them.

I have perceived that there is a need for a guide to the range of new and existing environmental law, designed to assist general practitioners in particular with an overview of the present state of the law and to equip them to deal with questions and problems which will frequently arise; for almost every client will now have to face some responsibility to the environment and will need help. The format of the book is aimed to help to reduce the time which frequently needs to be undertaken for research, which general practitioners and consultants can often ill afford. It is against this background that the work seeks to help and advise.

I would offer two main *caveats*. First, this is a handbook or short guide. It gives an outline of the law for busy practitioners but does not pretend to be a definitive treatise on the whole detail and minutiae relating to this rapidly expanding subject. Where appropriate, I have added signposts to further reading and study on specific aspects of the law. Secondly, the law relating to the environment is changing fast. Royal assent to the Environmental Protection Act 1990 was granted at the end of that year but at time of writing, the Act is only partly in force. However, large parts of the Act will come into force during 1992, sometimes only by reference to specific industries and processes. To take account of the likely changes in 1992, where possible reference has been made to impending new provisions. The law is as it is understood at 31 October 1991.

I owe some acknowledgements. I would like to thank my partners at Nicholson Graham & Jones for their positive help and support in promoting the concept of the handbook. I owe a debt to Claire Stevens and other colleagues who have word processed the whole volume with their typical professionalism.

October 1991 JOHN GARBUTT

Contents

xi

Contents xiii

Contents

Introduction

'In Britain we have well-developed systems for controlling and regulating pollution. The Water Act 1989 and the Environmental Protection Bill of 1990 include measures to strengthen the powers and resources of the various inspectorates. The government favours strong pollution inspectorates with clear remits to impose high quality standards.

The objects are:

To make our air cleaner and safer;
To achieve further improvements in the quality of our water and in the state of the North Sea and our other coastal waters;
To establish the levels of emissions that our air and waters can safely tolerate, and set up control mechanisms based on that;
To maintain and strengthen when necessary, controls over pollution from industry, including farming, and over dangerous chemicals and other substances; and
To provide the necessary incentives to industry to improve their environmental standards and develop clean technologies.'

This Common Inheritance: Britain's Environmental Strategy
(White Paper, September 1990, Cm 1200).

This is a small quote from a very large White Paper but it provides the essence of HM Government's policy intentions for the protection of the environment. To judge from current expressions of the other political parties it does not seem likely that environmental policies will be materially different as a result of any change of government.

One of the political parties to have made very little progress in the UK (and to have declined in parts of Europe) is the 'Green' party. No doubt in its early days its policies filled a vacuum, apparently because the major parties gave little obvious priority to the environment. In this they were well proved not to have accurately measured the mood of their electors but one suspects that the position has now been righted.

In volume and complexity, environmental legislation has now

1

taken a quantum leap. The major new statutes, the Water Act 1989 and the Environmental Protection Act 1990 introduce new concepts of responsibility and control in respect of which the lawyer, particularly the solicitor, will need to be well versed.

It is apparent that since all members of the human race are users of the main elements of the environment the legislation and policies concerning those elements will be bound to impact upon virtually every living soul. In a great many cases the impact will be sufficiently significant that the individual or organisation will require legal and other advice. New clients will be drawn not only from industry and commerce but from diverse occupations such as farming and forestry, hunting and fishing, finance and lending, transport and retailing, advertising and consumer affairs. The list seems endless.

Duties and liabilities so far as the environment are concerned will centre on a clear understanding, not only of the primary legislation but of the following other aspects.

(a) Statutory instruments.
(b) Government circulars.
(c) Other governmental statements of policy.
(d) Codes of practice, both from government and other agencies.
(e) Orders and policies of other agencies such as National Rivers Authority, HM Inspectorate of Pollution, Health and Safety Executive.
(f) European Commission pronouncements, where increasingly the Brussels influence is being felt (see Appendix E).
(g) Case law from Britain and elsewhere, particularly the European Court of Justice.

The role of the solicitor will be to keep his client abreast of:

(a) Rights and duties in regard to environmental law.
(b) The prohibitions and permissions associated with the use of natural resources and the handling of waste and other matter.
(c) The means by which authorisations, permissions and licences may be obtained.
(d) The prosper application of government controls. In this regard the solicitor is responsible to protect his client from excesses of government agencies.

(e) The civil and criminal law relating to the environment, the defences and penalties.

(f) The rights of the individual to complain to the controlling agency or to take individual or 'class' actions.

In short, the solicitor's duties and liabilities are to know in reasonable detail the law as it applies to his particular client and to ensure that that client is provided, first, with the protection to which he is entitled, secondly the keys with which to unlock the gates to solutions to his environmentally related problems and difficulties.

The practitioner, therefore, has a need for an understanding of the statutory and other law pertaining to the environment (Part I of this book). Secondly, he will need an appreciation of the procedures to obtain authorisations and approvals (Part II). Thirdly, he will need a reasonable understanding of civil and other liabilities and the rights of his client to use the civil courts for redress (Part III). Fourthly, an understanding of European community environmental policy and law is now crucial.

The consequences and influences on other parts of the law will be fully appreciated. Environmental law impinges, for example, upon company, commercial, litigation, property, safety and health and criminal sectors.

Nonetheless, there are difficulties:

(1) The legislation is now so extensive and complex that it is in danger of overtaking the average person's capacity to understand.

(2) Hitherto, training both before and subsequent to qualification tends not to meet the advancing need for environmental advice.

(3) It is a peculiarity of environmental law that there is a major intrusion of ministerial, local authority and other quasi-government agency policies. A compendium of knowledge of this usually intricate area is extremely difficult to secure.

(4) The European factor, as previously referred to.

This volume attempts to overcome some of these problems. It seeks to provide a general guide in handbook form to assist lawyers and others in a basic understanding of the burgeoning environmental law and to help the search for reliable advice. However, I should caution that this is but a general guide and deals largely with the law and policy in

England and Wales. It does not purport to be an exhaustive treatise on this wide subject. Readers will be guided to other material for a more detailed examination.

The first two parts of this book (Part I, The Statutory Codes, Part II, Applications for Approval) are written by reference to the specific environmental medium or category of impact eg water, air etc. In the case of noise, there being few examples at the present time where applications for approval are required, such application procedures are included in the Part I text.

PART I

The statutory codes

1 Water

ABSTRACTION

Responsibility for control of water abstraction is now vested in the National Rivers Authority (NRA) (Water Act 1989). The Water Act 1945 imposed restrictions and some control of abstraction, established a local organisation of water supplies, defining powers and duties of local authorities and water undertakers. To a large extent the provisions of the Act have been replaced by more recent legislation but obligations for the conservation and protection of water resources, particularly the prevention of waste still apply. The Act also provides a vehicle for by-laws to be made against the contamination of water, particularly that used for human consumption.

Water Resources Act 1963

The first Act comprehensively to control the abstraction and impounding of water was the Water Resources Act 1963. This Act established a subregional structure of authorities, tending to be based upon the main river basins. For the first time a formal and comprehensive restriction on the abstraction and impounding of water was imposed, although exceptions were provided for, both in the Act and by subsequent regulations. Otherwise, from June 1965, abstraction of water was forbidden except by licence. The prohibition included not only abstraction direct from a surface supply, eg river or lake, but also the construction of any well or borehole designed to withdraw water from underground (s23). In the main, exceptions were restricted to small abstractions (not exceeding 1,000 gallons), abstraction from an inland water for an occupier of contiguous land for use on that land either for domestic purposes or agriculture other

7

than spray irrigation. Similarly, abstraction from underground strata for domestic purpose was also excepted.

However, this right is further restricted by the Water Act 1989. Further exceptions permit abstraction for the purposes of land drainage or to prevent interference with mining, quarrying, engineering, building or similar operation. The restriction does not prevent the transfer of water from one inland water to another by a navigation, harbour or conservancy authority, nor to abstraction for use on a vessel for the purposes of fire fighting or for test purposes.

Water Resources Act 1991

In respect of all water legislation consolidating acts were passed during 1991. The law relating to the abstraction of water is now set out in the Water Resources Act 1991. It comes into force on 1st December 1991. Restrictions on abstraction will thereafter be governed by section 24 of the 1991 Act.

Licence of Right

Section 33 of the 1963 Act provided a special entitlement to a licence to abstract, known as the Licence of Right. Such licence was automatically granted to any person who was entitled to abstract water from a source of supply in a river authority area as at the date that this part of the Act came into force, or had a record of five years, continuous abstraction. The provision was of particular value to major industrial abstractors although an obligation to pay for such abstraction was established by Pt V of the 1963 Act, subsequently the Water Act 1973 but to be further modified by the Water Act 1989. Licences of right are presumed by the 1991 Act s65 and Schedule 7.

Impounding

The right to impound an inland water is restricted by s25 of the 1991 Act. Impounding includes the provision of a dam, weir or works for diversion. A licence to permit such works may be granted under s34 *et seq.*

Appeals etc.

There are provisions for an appeal against a decision, or lack of a decision of the NRA. In England, the appeal is made to the Secretary of State for the Environment. The decision by the Secretary of State is final, save that the validity of the decision as a matter of law may be questioned by s69 of the 1991 Act. The Secretary of State has power to call-in applications for his own decision (s41).

Miscellaneous matters

Abstractions or impounding without licence or in contravention of conditions of a licence are offences (WRA 1991 ss24-25).

There is an important additional benefit to the holder of a licence to abstract. Not only is he protected from any challenge to his right to abstract (subject to compliance with the licence and payment of charges) but he also owns a protected right in the sense that the NRA is liable not to derogate from that grant (1991 Act s60).

There are provisions for the transfer of licences eg on acquisition of land and facilities served by the abstraction and the holder may apply to revoke or vary. The NRA may also revoke or vary (s52) but in the event of any objection by the holder the proposal must be referred to the Secretary of State for adjudication. A local inquiry may follow.

Water Act 1989

This Act generated further significant changes to the water industry arising specifically from the government decision to privatise the water supply industry. However, excluded from the powers and responsibilities of the new water companies (generally having similar identities to their predecessors, the water authorities) was the regulatory function which now devolves to the National Rivers Authority. The overall effect of this is that whilst the water companies will remain the suppliers of water and sewerage services to individuals and organisations, regulatory control, ie the conservation and security of the proper use of water resources in England and Wales is now for the NRA to manage. A significant consequence of the split of the responsibilities for operation and regulation is the avoidance of any conflict of interest between the commercial implications of supplying water and sewerage services and proper, objective regulation, particularly of the latter. At first sight the regulatory policy of the NRA appears to be much firmer than that demonstrated by the former water authorities, with a greater readiness to prosecute and effect policing and monitoring strategies.

In its impact on commerce and industry generally the 1989 Act did not significantly alter the 1963 Act save that abstractions for domestic and agricultural use are more closely limited. It is noted that this will have a major effect upon large agricultural water users such as fish farms, now for the first time brought within the licensing requirements. As a concession to small generators of electricity (less than 5 megawatts) the abstraction of water for this purpose is not subject to charge.

Finally, in relation to water resources the WRA 1991 now provides a more detailed regime for the imposition of drought orders and for penalties for offences against such orders.

Charges

By section 123 of the 1991 Act the NRA is provided with powers to make a scheme imposing water resources charges both for licences under the Act and the abstraction of such water as is licensed. Schemes are published from time to time by the authority and are designed to fund water resources administration.

WATER POLLUTION

The main statutory responsibility for the prevention of water pollution in England and Wales now derives from the Water Act 1991, which from 1 December 1991 replaces the Control of Pollution Act 1974 provisions, except in Scotland and the Water Act 1989.

Earlier legislation

However, there remain some important remnants of earlier provisions. The Public Health Act 1936 identifies as a statutory nuisance (see below) ponds, ditches, etc which are prejudicial to health or a nuisance, or silted-up watercourses (s259). The Act also prohibits discharge to sewers of any matter likely to injure the sewer or prejudice the treatment and disposal of its contents, or any chemical refuse, heated water or stream, petroleum spirit or calcium carbide.

The Public Health (Drainage of Trade Premises) Act 1937 provides the legal basis upon which the occupier of any trade premises may, with the consent of the sewerage undertaker, discharge his trade effluent into the local sewers. It is the responsibility of the occupier of the trade premises to supply a notice to the undertaker specifying the nature or composition of the effluent, the maximum quantity to be discharged per day and the highest rate of discharge. There is a right in the undertaker to prohibit or regulate by conditions the nature, composition or quantity of the effluent to be discharged. In the event of dispute there is an appeal to the Secretary of State for the Environment.

The 1937 Act was substantially modified by the Public Health Act 1961 in that it permitted conditions to be imposed on consents and it gave power to vary those conditions. Another effect of the 1961 Act was to widen the definition of trade premises so as to include those used for agriculture or horticulture or for scientific research or experiment.

Water Resources Act 1991

The above legislation relates to the acceptance of effluent and pollution into the existing network of sewers. In the meantime preventative legislation was developing through the Rivers (Prevention of Pollution) Acts 1951 and 1961 but control is now largely embodied in the Water Resources Act 1991, consolidating the Water Act 1989 from 1 December 1991, which provides to the National Rivers Authority the closest and most complex system of control of pollution of water so far devised. To some extent the legislation arises as a consequence of EEC directives, eg purity of drinking water.

Important definitions

There are three elements to the Act's approach, viz 'controlled waters', 'water quality objectives' and the attainment of those objectives.

'Controlled waters' are defined in s104 as including lakes and ponds, rivers, estuaries, water in underground strata and certain coastal waters. Sections 82–84 impose on the Secretary of State a duty to classify the quality of controlled waters and to specify water quality objectives which it will be the responsibility of the NRA to achieve and maintain. The Secretary of State will retain an overall responsibility. What this means to business and the individual is that by s85 offences are committed if:

(a) any poisonous, noxious or polluting matter or any solid waste is permitted to enter any controlled waters;

(b) any matter other than trade effluent or sewage effluent is allowed to enter controlled waters through discharge to a drain or sewer in contravention of a relevant prohibition;

(c) any trade effluent or sewage effluent is permitted to be discharged to any controlled waters or into the sea outside controlled waters;

(d) generally any trade effluent or sewage effluent is discharged in contravention of any relevant prohibition from any building or plant onto any land or inland water.

A relevant prohibition relates to an NRA notice prohibiting any discharge or imposing any conditions for discharge or the discharge contains prescribed substances or concentrations.

Avoidance of the offence under s85 is achieved provided that any consent is granted under the terms of s88. This consent may be by various means but includes approvals under the 1991 Act, the Control of Pollution Act 1974 or Part I of the Environmental Protection Act 1990 (see Chapter 2).

Water protection zones and nitrate sensitive areas

A new concept within the 1991 Act relates to the pro-active powers contained in s93 and 94 (water protection zones and nitrate sensitive areas). Section 93 allows the Secretary of State (after consultation with the Minister of Agriculture) to prohibit or restrict the carrying on in a particular area of activities likely to result in the pollution of controlled waters. These are special powers which are made available to the Secretary of State to prevent or control the entry of any poisonous, noxious of polluting matter. The more specific power contained in s94 is similar. The power here is exercised by the Minister of Agriculture in England and is expressly to prevent or control the entry of nitrates into controlled waters which results from the use of land for agricultural purposes. Both the Secretary of State and the Minister have taken power to provide codes of good agricultural practice which have as one of their objectives a reconciliation of viable agriculture with the avoidance of pollution (s97).

Consent under Schedule 10

The NRA may impose conditions upon any consent which it decides to grant. Schedule 10, para (2) to the 1991 Act details the types of conditions that may be included. If the NRA decide that they wish to give a consent but representations or objections have been made in respect of the application then notice of the intention to grant consent must be given by the NRA to every person who made such representations or objections. This gives the opportunity for those persons to request the Secretary of State for the Environment to 'call in' the application for his own determination. In these circumstances a local inquiry may follow.

Revocation and alteration of consents

Schedule 10 also deals with the procedures whereby the NRA may secure revocation and alteration.

Charges for applications and consents

Schemes of charges in respect of applications and for consents (the latter on an annual basis) have been published and details will be made available by the NRA.

2 Air pollution and integrated pollution control

INTRODUCTION

Atmospheric pollution control has its roots in the long established Alkali etc. Works Regulation Act 1906, but was considerably modified by the Clean Air Acts 1956/68 and the Control of Pollution Act 1974. Certain other modifications derived from the Health and Safety at Work etc. Act 1974. All these acts are being swept away following the passage into law of the Environmental Protection Act 1990 Part I. However the new requirements of this act will be brought into force only gradually and in the meantime for existing processes the above provisions will continue to apply. At the stage where a new or substantially altered process is proposed then the new 1990 Act authorisation requirements will apply. So far as existing, unchanged processes are concerned a legislative transition will take place over a period planned to extend to 1995. Enforcement of the legislation is primarily the responsibility of HM Inspectorate of Pollution although direct policing is limited to the major industrial processes, the local public health authorities having the remaining duties. Processes are scheduled under the Act. Scheduled processes are now set out in the Heath and Safety (Emission into the Atmosphere) Regulations 1983 SI 1983 No 943 as amended by the Health and Safety (Emission into the Atmosphere) (Amendment) Regulations 1989 SI 1989 No 319. The combined effect of the legislation and the regulations is to require registration of all works and processes set out in the Schedule to the regulations of 1983 and 1989. Scheduled processes are required to be registered with HMIP and must comply with a requirement for 'best practicable means' to prevent the escape of noxious or offensive gases. Certification is required on an annual basis and regular inspection takes place. Usually for the major industries, proceedings may only be

14

taken by HMIP so that public health authorities' powers are restricted. However, nowadays many of the less significant processes, particularly those deriving from smaller and less 'high-tech' industry such as mineral works now devolve directly to the public health authority for enforcement, thereby reducing the load placed on HMIP.

The Clean Air Act 1956 makes an occupier of buildings emitting dark smoke guilty of an offence. 'Dark smoke' is specifically defined in s34 of the Act by reference to the ringelmann chart ie more than 40 per cent obscuration. However, the court is permitted to conclude that smoke is or is not dark smoke even if there has been no comparison with the chart. The combination of the 1956 and the 1968 Clean Air Acts makes clear that the offence may be committed from open sites.

A primary purpose of the 1956 Act was to ensure that new furnaces shall be, so far as is practicable, smokeless (s3) and that most larger furnaces should be fitted with arrestment plant to prevent the escape of grit and dust. It is an offence to allow the escape of such materials and, furthermore, to install such plant without formal approval by the local authority.

The main popular feature of the Clean Air Act 1956 was to set in place provisions for local authorities to declare districts smoke control areas. This was in response to serious smoke related air pollution problems in many cities in the 1950s. The effect of the establishment of a smoke control area is to prohibit the emission of any smoke but subject to specific exemptions and limitations. However certain authorised fuels are permitted to be burned – tending to be of the 'smokeless' variety.

Section 16 of the 1956 Act specifies the emission of smoke as a potential public nuisance under the Public Health Act 1936 which in turn triggers the procedures under that Act for abatement and prohibition.

The Clean Air Act 1968 had the effect of strengthening the 1956 Act in regard to the prohibition of dark smoke and the emission of grit and dust from furnaces.

Whilst the air pollution provisions of the Health and Safety at Work etc. Act 1974 mainly relate to work place conditions there are imposed general duties on persons in control of certain premises to prevent harmful emissions into atmosphere (s5). However, by and large the obligations correspond to the earlier legislation.

Control of Pollution Act 1974

The Control of Pollution Act 1974 had little effect upon the earlier legislation so far as air pollution was concerned except that it provided powers:

    (a) to regulate the composition of motor fuel so as to reduce air pollution,

    (b) to similarly regulate the sulphur content of furnace or engine oil.

    (c) to prevent cable burning except under proper conditions.

    (d) to require information about air pollution for the purposes of publishing information to the public. There are certain protections in regard to the demand for information if to give it would prejudice commercial secrets, be contrary to public interest or be unduly costly and difficult to collect.

INTEGRATED POLLUTION CONTROL AND AIR POLLUTION CONTROL BY LOCAL AUTHORITIES (ENVIRONMENTAL PROTECTION ACT 1990)

This Act was passed in November 1990. In relation to industrial processes which have a major potential for pollution entirely new systems of control known as integrated pollution control will be instituted. Processes perceived as having less significance in pollution terms will be under the control of local authorities but only so far as air pollution is concerned. Processes and substances the subject of Part I of the Act are set out in The Environmental Protection (Prescribed Processes and Substances) Regulations 1991. SI 1991 No 472.

Integrated pollution control

Strictly speaking, the concept of integrated pollution control (IPC) is not a new one. There has always been a natural propensity in the systems of control through town and country planning, public health and pollution control to achieve the least offensive consequences of pollution by industrial and other activities. Thus the Alkali Acts have progressively reduced atmospheric pollution in favour of recycling of gases and particulate matter leading to the disposal of the residue on land. Furthermore, the disposal of cooling waters to rivers and seas has been reduced in favour of discharges to atmosphere through cooling towers. Recycling and energy factors link to this concept.

What is integrated pollution control?

The system arises through a scheme of authorisation, control and enforcement of processes capable of causing pollution to the environment. A process falls into this category if it releases to air, water or land substances which are capable of causing harm to man or any other living organism supported by the environment (s1). The definition is exceedingly wide and likely to provide fertile ground for interpretative disputes in the courts and through the public inquiry procedures set up by the Act.

A process will not be caught by the IPC requirements until it is prescribed by the Secretary of State.

Preliminary

The power to prescribe processes is vested in the Secretary of State by s2. The Secretary of State will by regulations prescribe any description of process in respect of which an authorisation is required under s6. Regulations are intended to frame the description of the process by reference to characteristics, or the area, or other circumstances in which the process is carried on, or the description of the person undertaking it.

It is intended by virtue of the regulations to assign the more complex and highly technical processes for control by Her Majesty's Inspectorate of Pollution (HMIP). However, a wide range of processes is intended to be designated for control by local public health authorities in England and Wales. To some extent the division of responsibilities is already established by virtue of the Alkali Acts and the Health and Safety at Work etc Act 1974 but the main difference in this area is that local authorities will now have prior authorisation duties which hitherto have not been required by the earlier legislation. A general list of these processes is in Appendices A and B.

Quality targets

Section 3 provides the basis for targets at which the Secretary of State will aim. The section will enable him to establish standards, objectives or requirements in relation to prescribed processes of particular substances. There are wide ranging options for the Secretary of State who would seem to have all necessary powers to:

(1) limit the concentration, the amount or the amount in any period of a substance to be released from a prescribed process;
(2) limit any characteristic of the substance to be released;
(3) prescribe standard requirements for measurements;
(4) prescribe other standards or requirements as to any aspect of the process.

Associated with these wide powers is the additional power to make regulations applying different standards to different processes, industries, localities or circumstances. Established in this section is the right (ss(5)) to secure a progressive improvement in the quality objectives and quality standards and the Secretary of State's plans may be revised from time to time to accommodate such improvement.

Powers of HMIP and local authorities

The division of powers between HMIP and the local public health authorities is determined by s4. In respect of HMIP there are effectively no geographical limits within England and Wales. Local public health authorities will be responsible for all processes carried on within their area but the functions applicable to such processes are exercisable in respect of air pollution and not to any other environmental medium, ie land or water. Special provision has been made in the case of mobile plant where the appropriate public health authority will be that in whose area the person carrying on the mobile process has his principal place of business.

The Secretary of State has taken power under s4 to transfer responsibilities normally exercised by a local authority to HMIP but in these cases the limits of control, ie in respect of air pollution only, do not change.

The local authority

The local authority is defined in the section to mean (i) in Greater London, the London Borough Council, the Common Council of the City of London, the Sub-treasurer of the Inner Temple and the

Under-treasurer of the Middle Temple; (ii) outside Greater London the district council and the council of the Isles of Scilly. There is a modification in those cases where by the Public Health (Control of Disease) Act 1984 a port health authority has been constituted for any port health district. In this case, the responsibilities of Pt I, normally assigned to local authority, will be assigned to the port health authority.

Authorisations

Section 6 establishes a specific prohibition on any person carrying on a prescribed process (after the prescribed date) except by virtue of an authorisation granted either by HMIP or the local authority and in accordance with the conditions of that authorisation.

Schedule 1 to the Act sets out some of the procedural requirements (see Chapter 8). The responsibility on the enforcing authority is either to grant the authorisation on the application made, subject to conditions, or refuse it. The enforcing authority is expressly forbidden to grant an application if it considers that the applicant will be unable to carry on the process so as to comply with the conditions which would normally be included in the authorisation.

Reviews of authorisations

It is to be noted that the enforcing authority will have a responsibility from time to time but not less frequently than once in every four years to carry out a review of the conditions of the authorisation. Indeed, this period may be changed by regulations made by the Secretary of State.

Applications for authorisations

Schedule 1 to the Act requires applications for authorisations to be made in such a manner as are to be prescribed in regulations (see the Environmental Protection (Applications, Appeals and Registers) Regulations 1991. SI 1991 No 507). They will be accompanied by a fee and the usual requirement will be for advertisement, again as specified in regulations. The authority is entitled to all relevant information which must be supplied within a specified timetable and in the event of the absence of information then the application may not proceed.

There will be obligations on the enforcing authority to consult with prescribed persons and to consider any responses. Again, regulations will prescribe who will be the consultees. Besides those specifically consulted, all representations made within the time period are required to be considered by the authority in making a decision. There is a 28-day period for consultees and others wishing to make representations, starting respectively from the date on which notice of application was given or advertisement made.

In normal circumstances the enforcing authority has four months to make a decision on the application, or such longer period as may be agreed with the applicant. There are similar deemed refusal provisions as exist with planning applications.

Call-in powers

The Secretary of State may 'call in' any application for his own decision and in those circumstances a local inquiry may be held whereby the applicant and the authority have a right of audience. The local inquiry must be held if either the applicant or the local authority require it. In the circumstances of 'call in' the Secretary of State will apparently not make the decision himself but give directions to the authority as to whether or not to grant the application and as to the conditions to be attached to any authorisation.

Conditions of authorisations

Assuming that an authorisation is to be granted then s7 is the operative provision for conditions of that authorisation. At this stage in the system there is a divergence between the IPC procedures for authorisation operated by HMIP and the air pollution control responsibilities of the local authority. They are, therefore, dealt with separately.

IPC

Section 7 sets out objectives (sub-s(2)) as follows:

(a) That in carrying on the prescribed process best available techniques not entailing excessive cost (BATNEEC) will be used for preventing the release of substances prescribed for any environmental medium into that medium or, where that is not practicable, reducing the release to a minimum and for rendering harmless any such substances which are so released and for rendering harmless any other substances which might cause harm if released into any environmental medium. The basic requirement on prescribed processes will be to employ BATNEEC. This definition is examined (on page 23).

(b) Compliance with any directions by the Secretary of State in pursuance of any obligations of the UK under European Community or international law relating to environmental protection.

(c) Compliance with any limits or requirements and achievement of quality standards or objectives prescribed by the Secretary of State.

(d) Compliance with any requirements of a plan for general improvement made under the provisions of s3(5) which relates to total release limits, quotas etc.

(e) Where IPC applies (so that the process is designated for central control) and where it is likely to involve the release of substances into more than one environmental medium, then the BATNEEC obligation extends to minimising pollution caused to the environment taken as a whole by the releases, having regard to the best practicable environmental option (BPEO) available as respects the released substances.

BPEO

In regard to IPC processes, the function of HMIP will be to authorise only such processes which produce the optimum pollution control system, ie BPEO. Thus, discharges ultimately to land may be preferred as the least damaging environmentally when compared with discharges, eg to air and/or water. The implications of the BPEO system seem to be extremely wide and may well lead to *de novo* appraisals of process systems. Environmental assessments are likely to be an invariable requirement of any application for an authorisation made to HMIP and the testing of one method of environmental control against another will be part of these. The combination of BATNEEC and BPEO is seen as giving an impetus to the potential for recycling waste materials and effluent.

Local air pollution control

The objectives as described in sub-s(2) of s7 are largely the same for local authority control except as regards the BPEO obligation. Since local authorities will only be dealing with relatively simple air pollution consequences of the processes under their control, the government has not seen it as necessary to apply the integrated control assessments which will be the responsibility of HMIP.

Conditions

The enforcing authority must meet the above objectives in setting conditions of the authorisation. It additionally must take into account any directions given by the Secretary of State (s7(3)) and must impose any other conditions as may be appropriate. However, there is a prohibition against the imposition of any condition which has the purpose only of securing the health of persons at work. This is intended to avoid duplication of control already exercised under Pt I of the Health and Safety at Work etc Act 1974.

Section 7(4) makes clear that there is implied in every authorisation a general condition requiring BATNEEC to be used to meet the objectives above mentioned.

Sub-section (8) imposes further obligations in the form of conditions of an authorisation. An authorisation for carrying on a prescribed process may include conditions imposing limits on the amount or composition of any substance produced by or utilised in the process in any period and require advance notification of any proposed change.

Avoidance of duplication of controls

Section 28 contains some important provisions which seek to avoid conflict between different regimes of statutory control. These include:

(1) That no condition may be attached to an authorisation to regulate the final disposal by deposit in or on land of controlled waste (this will be dealt with under Pt II of the Act and is currently dealt with by the Control of Pollution Act 1974). However, the enforcing authority must notify the waste regulation authority for the area where the process is to be

carried on of the fact that the process involves the final disposal of controlled waste by deposit in or on land. It is to be noted that the authority to be notified is not necessarily that where the controlled waste is actually disposed of.

(2) In circumstances where an authorisation is required under Pt I and also under the Radioactive Substances Act 1960, and different obligations are imposed, the Pt I provision will not be binding on the person carrying on the process.

(3) In circumstances where the prescribed process designated for central control includes the release of substances into controlled waters under the Water Act 1991 then the National Rivers Authority has certain powers of veto. These are that the enforcing authority shall not grant an authorisation if the NRA certifies that the release to water will cause or contribute to a failure to achieve a water quality objective and in any authorisation granted the NRA may require conditions to be imposed.

(4) In the above circumstances the NRA may also intervene to vary conditions of an authorisation if they see this as appropriate.

Allowing that the new BPEO provisions give HMIP new statutory responsibilities in regard not only to air but also to water and land, it is difficult to escape the conclusion that the relationship with other authorities and their powers in respect of the other environmental media could be uneasy, at least in the early stages of the new IPC control system. Section 28 of the 1990 Act attempts to deal with the more obvious interface problems but bearing in mind that there are bound to be conflicts between choices for disposal to different types of media, it seems more than likely that BPEO solutions will not always be universally acceptable to such as the NRA and the local authorities responsible for the disposal of waste on land. Industry might well find itself somewhat caught in the cross-fire. However, proposals for a co-ordination of those functions in an Environmental Protection Agency should materially assist.

BATNEEC

Section 7 is also the vehicle for defining the necessary and appropriate components of BATNEEC. In relation to a process these include (in addition to references to any technical means and technology) references to the number, qualifications, training and supervision of persons employed in the process and the design, construction, layout and maintenance of buildings in which it is carried on. Sub-s(11) places a duty on the enforcing authorities to have regard to any guidance issued to them by the Secretary of State for the purposes of this section, with particular regard to the techniques and environmental options that are appropriate for any description of prescribed process.

A general guidance note on the meaning of BATNEEC is in Appendix C. However it will be noted that whilst some assistance is available in regard to the interpretation of best available techniques, the note is shy on the much more difficult element 'not entailing excessive costs'. A number of guides have now been issued by the Department of the Environment, notably 'Integrated Pollution. A Practical Guide'. The approach to NEEC will be likely to be different depending upon whether the process to be authorised is a new one or an existing one. It is to be anticipated that the courts will be called upon to assist with interpretation but as a general guideline it would seem that the presumption that best available techniques must be used can properly be modified where the costs of applying those techniques would be excessive in relation to the nature of the industry and the environmental protection to be achieved. Economic considerations to be taken into account may be temporary or more prolonged, for example where a particular industry is in recession or suffering from individual economic difficulties. However there is a limit to the extent to which overriding economic considerations can interfere with the requirement for BAT and this will depend upon the circumstances in each case.

Process guidance notes

The DOE and Welsh office are currently preparing and issuing a series of specific guidance notes on individual processes for consultation with HMIP, local authorities and other interested bodies, particularly industry. They are described as being based on the state of knowledge and understanding of such processes, their potential impact on the environment and the available control techniques at time of publication. The guidance is to be updated 'regularly to reflect changes in knowledge and understanding'. However, it has already been acknowledged that advances in technology may move faster than the revision of the guidance notes. Furthermore, the notes will not take into account individual process characteristics, eg location. This means that on occasions the choice of BATNEEC may not be fully identified by the extant guidance note hitherto relevant.

In addition to the process guidance notes industry sector guidance notes IPR 1 to 5 have also been issued. These are more general assessments of five sectors of industry likely to be most affected by Part I of the Act. They are fuel and power, metals, minerals, chemicals and waste disposal.

Finally the Department of the Environment, the Scottish office and the Welsh office are issuing a further set of Secretary of State's guidance notes which are intended to be addressed to local authorities who have their own responsibilities under Part I of the Act. These deal with not only general questions such as procedures, enforcement etc. but will also refer to specific industries and processes the responsibility of local government.

Fees and charges

A scheme of fees and charges is prescribed by the Secretary of State and s8 provides for an up-dating of the scheme from time to time. Charges will be imposed for (a) applications for authorisations (b) variations (c) renewals.

There is power for the Secretary of State to make separate charging schemes for HMIP and local systems of authorisation and it is proposed that this is what will happen. Schemes including different fees for different applicants, circumstances and localities can be established. However, the overall aim is that the system of fees and charges shall be self-sufficient by reference to the expenditure attributable to authorisations.

A failure to pay a charge renders an authorisation liable to revocation.

TRANSFER, VARIATION AND REVOCATION (ss9–12)

Transfer

An authorisation may be transferred on a change of any authorised holder. The responsibility to notify the enforcing authority is on the transferee who must give notice of the fact within 21 days. From date of transfer the transferee takes on all the obligations of the authorisation and the conditions (s9).

Variation

Sections 10 and 11 lay down procedures applying where variation of conditions of authorisations are required to be made. An enforcing authority may vary an authorisation at any time and must do so if this is required by eg a change of circumstances in the conditions laid down by s7.

Variation by enforcing authority

The procedure is triggered by the service under s10 of a variation notice on the holder of the authorisation which must specify the variations decided upon and the dates on which these variations are to take effect. The notice must also require the holder of the authorisation, within a specified period, to identify to the authority what action (if any) he proposes to take in response to the variation. A holder may be required to pay a fee, again within a specified period. In the circumstances where the enforcing authority is of the opinion that the variation will involve a substantial change in the process, the opinion must be notified to the holder and such holder will be required to advertise the change.

'Substantial change' is defined in sub-s(7) as being 'a substantial change in the substances released from the process or in the amount or any other characteristic of any substance so released'. A power has been taken for the Secretary of State to give directions to identify what constitutes a substantial change.

Variation by holder of authorisation

The procedure for variation where the holder wishes to make any relevant change in the process is slightly different. It is to be noted that the requirements of s11 are dictated by any need to make a 'relevant change' in the prescribed process. This is defined as 'a change in the manner of carrying on the process which is capable of altering the substances released from the process or of affecting the amount or any other characteristic of any substance so released'.

In the case of a relevant change, the holder must:

(a) notify the enforcing authority, and
(b) request a determination of the following matters, viz:
  (i) whether the proposed change would involve a breach of any condition of the authorisation;
  (ii) if there is no breach, whether the authority would be likely to vary the conditions of the authorisation as a result of the change;
  (iii) if it would involve a breach, whether the authority would consider varying the conditions of the authorisation to enable the change to be made;
  (iv) whether the change would involve a substantial change in the manner in which the process is being carried on.

If the enforcing authority decides that no substantial change has taken place but that a variation of the authorisation should follow, then the holder must be notified of the variations to be considered and the holder must then apply for such variation to enable him to make the proposed change.

Alternatively, if the enforcing authority decides that a proposed change would be a substantial one then the same procedure follows but, in addition, the holder must advertise the change in the prescribed manner.

On receiving the application for variation, the enforcing authority may refuse the application or vary the conditions as it thinks fit and in the latter case must serve a variation notice on the holder of the authorisation. An appropriate fee will be applied here.

Revocation of authorisation

Revocation of an authorisation is also available to an enforcing authority by virtue of s12. The authority would deal with this where it has reason to believe that an authorised process had not been carried on for at least a period of 12 months. Twenty-eight days' notice of revocation must be given but there is a power to withdraw the notice or vary the date at the discretion of the enforcing authority.

ENFORCEMENT AND OFFENCES

Powers of enforcement include the right to serve enforcement or prohibition notices.

Enforcement notice

These notices flow from contravention of any condition of an authorisation or the authority's anticipation that contravention is likely. The notice is required to specify that the authority believes that the condition is contravened or about to be contravened, must identify the matters representing the contravention and the steps that must be taken to remedy, as well as the period within which action must be taken. The Secretary of State may give directions here (s13).

Prohibition notice

The prohibition notice is a more serious matter and arises where the enforcing authority believes that an authorised process involves an imminent risk of serious pollution of the environment. Contravention of a condition of an authorisation is not a condition precedent. This notice must state the authority's opinion, specify the risk involved in the process and the steps that must be taken to remove it, as well as the period within which action is to be taken. Additionally, the notice must direct that the authorisation shall, either wholly or as to the extent specified in the notice, cease to authorise the carrying on of the process. This situation persists until the notice is withdrawn. The notice may, if it applies to part only of the process, impose conditions in carrying on the remaining part. Powers of direction are again available to the Secretary of State. Once the enforcing authority is satisfied that the steps required by the notice have been taken, then it may serve notice withdrawing the prohibition notice (s14).

APPEALS

Section 15 deals with rights of appeal in respect of Pt I of the Act in the following circumstances:

(a) on refusal of the grant of an authorisation;
(b) on receipt of an authorisation with unsatisfactory condition;

    (c) on refusal of a variation;
    (d) on revocation of an authorisation;
    (e) on receipt of a variation notice;
    (f) on receipt of an enforcement notice;
    (g) on receipt of a prohibition notice;

In all cases, the appeal is to the Secretary of State.

The procedure for an appeal in each case requires the Secretary of State either to refer the matter to a person appointed by him for the purpose or to delegate the decision to an appointee. This procedure appears to be similar to that now applied in respect of planning appeals. The appeal will be required to be advertised and, if either party to the appeal so requests, a hearing (as opposed to an inquiry) shall be held. Part of this hearing or all of it may be held in private as the 'inspector' decides.

Appeal powers of the Secretary of State

The powers of the Secretary of State in determining an appeal under (a) to (d) above extend to:

    (a) affirmation of the decision;
    (b) direction to the enforcing authority to grant the authorisation or to vary;
    (c) quashing of unsatisfactory conditions, and
    (d) quashing of any revocation.

Save in respect of the affirmation of the decision, directions may be given as to the appropriate conditions to be attached.

In the case of an appeal against a variation, enforcement, or prohibition notice ((e) to (g) above), the Secretary of State may either quash or affirm the notice and in the latter case he may do this either in the original form or with modifications.

Whilst in some cases an appeal will have the effect of suspending any revocation of an authorisation this will not apply where a variation, enforcement or prohibition notice has been served.

POWERS OF INSPECTORS (ss16–18)

Inspectors appointed either by the Secretary of State or the local authority have a wide range of powers to administer and enforce the legislation (s17). These are exercisable in relation to premises (a) on which a prescribed process is or is believed to be carried on, and (b) to premises on which a prescribed process has been carried on (whether or not the process was a prescribed process when it was being carried on), the condition of which is believed to be such as to give rise to a risk of serious pollution of the environment.

The powers of the inspector are:

    (a) to enter at any reasonable time where there is an immediate risk of serious pollution and to take with him any duly authorised persons, including a constable if serious obstruction is anticipated, and any equipment or materials relevant to the power of entry ie measuring equipment etc;

    (b) to make an examination and investigation;

    (c) to require premises or anything in them to be left undisturbed so long as is reasonably necessary for examination or investigation;

    (d) to take measurements, photographs and other records as well as samples;

    (e) to require the dismantling of any article or the testing of any substance where such have been thought to be likely to cause pollution of the environment and to take possession if necesary;

    (f) to require information from relevant person as well as records;

    (g) to require any person to give facilities and assistance within that person's control and responsibility;

    (h) any other power conferred by regulations.

Protection of process operators and others

Enshrined in s17 are various protections. For example, the power to dismantle equipment or subject substances to tests may not be undertaken without giving the opportunity for the person in charge of the premises to be present and in these circumstances the inspector is obliged to consult with all appropriate persons to ascertain dangers in the action which he proposes. The taking away of any equipment or sample requires the inspector to give notice to the responsible person or leave conspicuously a notice sufficiently identifying what was taken away and, where practicable, leaving a sample.

In so far as anyone has given information to an inspector, that information is privileged and not admissible in evidence in any subsequent proceedings. Furthermore, there is no right in an inspectorate to compel the production of any document which can be the subject of legal professional privilege.

Emergencies

Section 18 deals with the circumstances where the inspector has reasonable cause to believe that there is imminent danger of serious harm caused by an article or substance which he finds on any premises. He has power to seize the article or substance and cause it to be rendered harmless. However, before he may do this he is required to separate a sample and give it to a responsible person at the premises in question. The sample must be marked in a manner sufficient to identify it. Furthermore, as soon as possible after seizure and the rendering harmless of the article or substances a written report must be prepared by the inspector (and signed) identifying the circumstances. A copy of the report must go to the responsible person and to the owner of the article or substance. Service on the owner is satisfied if the inspector cannot reasonably ascertain the name or address, by service on the responsible person.

INFORMATION

Section 19 provides for the obtaining of information and is in two parts. In the first part the Secretary of State may by notice in writing to an enforcing authority require information about the discharge of its functions. In the second part, the Secretary of State or any of the enforcing authorities may require any person to give information as may be specified in a notice which the authority thinks it reasonably requires.

OFFENCES

The offence provision is s23. Offences arise if any person:

    (a) fails to comply with the requirements of authorisations under s6;

(b) fails to give notice under s9 (transfer of authorisation);
(c) fails to comply with an enforcement or prohibition notice;
(d) fails without reasonable excuse to comply with the require-
     ments of an inspector or prevents another person from doing
     so;
(e) intentionally obstructs an inspector in the exercise of his
     duty;
(f) fails without reasonable excuse to comply with a notice
     requiring information;
(g) makes a false or misleading statement;
(h) intentionally makes a false entry in any record required to be
     kept under a condition of an authorisation;
(i) forges or uses an authorisation with intent to deceive;
(j) falsely pretends to be an inspector;
(k) fails to comply with a court order made under s26 (see
     below).

Penalties are substantial, on summary conviction up to £20,000 and
on indictment to an unlimited fine or imprisonment for up to two
years, or both. Additionally there is a right for the enforcing authority
to go to the High Court if the proceedings in the lower court for failure
to comply with a prohibition notice or enforcement notice are
inadequate.

Supplementary powers are available under s26 where there is a
conviction for an offence under s23(1)(a) – failure to obtain authorisation or comply with conditions, and 23(1)(c) – failure to comply with
any enforcement or prohibition notice. In addition to any punish-
ment, the court may also order steps to be taken to remedy the offence
but only if those steps are within the power of the offender to remedy.
Furthermore, by s27 HMIP, but apparently not the local authority,
can obtain the authorisation of the Secretary of State to take steps to
remedy harm and to recover the cost from the offender.

STANDARDS OF PROOF

Section 25 has an effect upon the normal standards of onus of proof. In
circumstances where proceedings are taken against a person for
failure to use BATNEEC it is for the accused to prove that no better
available technique not entailing excessive cost was appropriate.

Further, the absence of an entry in a record required to be kept is admissible as evidence that the conditon relevant to the record has not been observed.

PUBLICITY

Public registers of information are required to be kept by s20 of the Act. In respect of prescribed processes, the following information needs to be registered as appropriate by HMIP and the local authority:

(a) applications for authorisations made to the authority;
(b) authorisations granted or in respect of which the authority has functions under Pt I;
(c) variation, enforcement and prohibition notices issued by that authority;
(d) revocations of authorisations effected by that authority;
(e) appeals;
(f) convictions (as may be prescribed);
(g) information obtained or furnished in pursuance of conditions of authorisations or under any provision of Pt I;
(h) directions given to the authority by the Secretary of State;
(i) any other matters as prescribed.

Local authorities (but not port health authorities) are also required to maintain in their register prescribed particulars of appropriate information contained in the register kept by HMIP as it relates to the carrying on in the authority's area of prescribed processes for which the HMIP has the responsibility.

CONFIDENTIALITY

Some information may be excluded from the register but the register must make this clear. Exclusions arise under ss21 and 22 in cases where the Secretary of State is satisfied that the information would affect national security. Furthermore by s22 no information relating to the affairs of any individual or business may be included in a register without the consent of the individual or business if it is commercially confidential and not specially required to be included in the register (see below, sub-s(7)). Information will only be regarded as commercially confidential if the authority so determines or if the Secretary of State determines after an appeal. Sub-section (7) is important in that it gives to the Secretary of State the right to override commercial confidentiality if, in his view, the public interest requires that information to be included. Commercial confidentiality only lasts for four years unless the supplier of the information requests a further exclusion and the authority must then decide whether or not that is the case. Commercial confidentiality arises if publication would prejudice to an unreasonable degree the commercial interests of the individual or person.

3 Waste on land

THE LEGISLATIVE FRAMEWORK

Until the coming into force of Pt II of the Environmental Protection Act 1990 (see later page 41) the main legislative provision appropriate to the control of waste on land is the Control of Pollution Act 1974. However, there are other provisions of which the following may be appropriate in certain circumstances.

Public Health Act 1936

These provisions mainly relate to powers for the local public health authority to abate nuisances and/or to require an owner or occupier of premises to remove noxious matter, manure etc in an urban district (s79 to 80). Procedures are based upon the statutory nuisance provisions of the Act and now replaced by Part III of the Environmental Protection Act 1990.

Section 259 of the 1936 Act specifies that the definition of statutory nuisance for the purposes of Pt III of the 1936 Act is to include:

(a) Any pond, pool, ditch, gutter or water course which is so foul or in such a state as to be prejudicial to health or a nuisance.

(b) Any part of a water-course not being a part ordinarily navigated by vessels employed in the carriage of goods by water which is so choked or silted up as to obstruct or impede the proper flow of water and thereby to cause a nuisance, or give rise to conditions prejudicial to health. However, in regard to this paragraph there is a proviso that nothing in the sub-section shall be deemed to impose any liability on any person other than the person by whose act or default the nuisance arises or continues.

35

Public Health Act 1961

Section 34 of this Act provides a power to the local authority where there is on any land in the open air in their area any rubbish which is seriously detrimental to the amenities of the neighbourhood. In these circumstances the local authority may take steps for removing the rubbish in the interests of amenity. A necessary pre-condition to action is that notice shall be served on the owner and occupier of the land stating the steps proposed to be taken by the local authority and the particulars of counter-action available to the person upon whom the notice is served. That person and any other person having an interest in the land may within 28 days from the service of the notice either serve a counter-notice on the local authority stating that he intends to take those steps himself or appeal to the magistrates' court on the grounds that the local authority was not justified in concluding that action should be taken under the section or that the steps proposed to be taken are unreasonable.

Section 34(3) goes on to provide that the local authority is required to take no further action in the matter unless the person who served the counter-notice fails within the local authorities interpretation of a reasonable time to begin to take the steps indicated in the notice or fails to make adequate progress to completion.

The definition of 'rubbish' is dealt with in sub-s(5) and includes rubble, waste paper, crockery and metal and any other kind of refuse (including organic matter) but does not include material accumulated for or in the course of any business or waste deposited in accordance with a disposal licence in force under Pt I of the Control of Pollution Act 1974.

Control of Pollution Act 1974

The 1974 Act brought into force a new system of control of waste disposal. With certain subsidiary legislation this remains the appropriate and current Act but this will be replaced by the Environmental Protection Act 1990, Part II, probably starting in 1992. The incineration of and other treatment of waste is also the subject of Part I of that Act (see Chapter 2).

The Definition of 'waste'

Waste is defined by s30(1) as including:

   (a) any substance which constitutes a scrap material or an effluent or other unwanted surplus substance arising from the application of any process and

   (b) any substance or article which requires to be disposed of as being broken, warn out, contaminated or otherwise spoiled.

but does not include a substance which is an explosive within the meaning of the Explosives Act 1875.

It is to be noted that for the purposes of offences under Pt I of the 1974 Act 'waste' is interpreted by reference to the person disposing of the material. Therefore, an occupier needs a licence for the disposal even of top soil from a building site and may be convicted of an offence of tipping this material on another's land without a licence (*Long* v *Brooke* [1980] Crim LR 109).

For the purposes of specific controls under the 1974 'waste' has a complicated definition with three separate sub-divisions.

'Controlled waste' under the 1974 Act means household, industrial and commercial waste or any such waste. Three separate definitions are to be found in s30(3) as follows:

   (a) household waste consists of waste from a private dwelling or residential home or from premises forming part of a university or school or other educational establishment or forming part of a hospital or nursing home;

   (b) industrial waste consists of waste from any factory within the meaning of the Factories Act 1961 and any premises occupied by a body corporate established by or under any enactment for the purpose of carrying on under national ownership any industry or part of an industry or any undertaking, excluding waste from any mine or quarry.

   (c) commercial waste consists of waste from premises used wholly or mainly for the purposes of a trade or business or the purposes of sport, recreation or entertainment excluding

      (i) household and industrial waste and

      (ii) waste from any mine or quarry and waste from premises used for agriculture within the meaning of the Agriculture Act 1947 and

(iii) waste of any other description prescribed for the
purposes of this paragraph.

Powers have been taken under s30(4) for the Secretary of State to
modify these definitions by reference to a specific type of waste. Some
modifications have been secured by the Collection and Disposal of
Waste Regulations 1988 and the Control of Pollution (Landed Ships
Waste) Regulations 1987.

Offences

The unlicensed disposal of controlled waste is an offence (s3) regarded
as of sufficient seriousness that the worst cases can attract terms of
imprisonment of up to five years and/or unlimited fines. The offences
extend to:

(a) depositing controlled waste on any land or causing or knowingly permitting the deposit; or

(b) the use of any plant or equipment or causing or knowingly
permitting such use in the disposal of controlled waste or
dealing with controlled waste.

There is a second level of contravention which attracts the serious
penalties. This arises where the waste in question is poisonous,
noxious or polluting, is deposited on land in a way likely to give rise to
an environmental hazard and is left there, leading to the reasonable
assumption of abandonment or disposal.

Licences

It follows from the above that disposal of controlled waste requires a
licence (s5) issued in England by the county council and in Wales by
the district council (although other arrangements exist for London
and the metropolitan authorities). The waste disposal authority is
bound to grant the application (provided that it is in order) unless
rejection is necessary for the purpose of preventing pollution of water
or danger to public health. A planning permission for the activity
must exist under the Town and Country Planning Act 1990 or its
predecessors before a disposal licence may be granted. The licence
may impose a series of conditions (s6). The Secretary of State for the
Environment has sponsored publications and codes of practice for

guidance of the controlling authorities and licencees. (See various waste management papers obtainable from the Department of the Environment/HMSO.) Licences and conditions thereof may be varied and revoked, transferred and relinquished (s7 and 8).

Administration of licensed sites

Supervision of licensed activities is the responsibility of the authority issuing the licence (s9(1)). The authority has a duty (a) to take the steps needed so that the licensed activities do not cause pollution of water or danger to public health or become seriously detrimental to the amenities of the locality affected by the activity and (b) to ensure that the conditions of the licence are complied with.

Enforcement powers

In order to perform the above duties there is power for an officer of the authority duly authorised in writing to take emergency steps and, if necessary to do so, to carry out work on the relevant land and on any plant or equipment to which the licence relates (s9(2)). By sub-s(3) any expenditure incurred as a result of taking the above mentioned action may be recovered from the holder of the disposal licence, or, if that licence has been revoked or cancelled, from the person who last held the licence. However, the holder or last holder may escape responsibility for payment if he shows either that there was no emergency requiring any work or that the expenditure was unnecessary.

Further enforcement powers appear in sub-s(4) in circumstances where the disposal authority concludes that a condition of the licence is not being complied with. Whilst this is an offence punishable under s3 and/or s6(3), nonetheless it is open to the disposal authority to serve on the licence holder a notice requiring him to comply with the condition within a timescale specified. Failure to comply with the condition as directed entitles the disposal authority to revoke the licence, again within a timescale specified in the notice.

Appeals

Appeals lie to the Secretary of State for the Environment:

    (a) where an application for a disposal licence or modification has been rejected;
    (b) against the conditions of a disposal licence;
    (c) against the terms of a modification of conditions of a disposal licence;
    (d) against the revocation of a disposal licence (s10).

The procedure for appeals is dealt with in the Collection and Disposal of Waste Regulations 1988 (SI 1988 No 819).

Despite these regulations procedures for dealing with the appeal are not specified in detail. Experience of the small number of appeals so far undertaken shows that the Secretary of State may decide to hold a public inquiry using powers under s290 of the Local Government Act 1972. However, by s19(1) of the 1974 Act the Secretary of State's powers to determine the appeal are achieved by a direction that the decision is to be altered and requiring the waste disposal authority to give effect to the determination.

Procedure on modification

In circumstances where there is an appeal against modification of conditions of a disposal licence or against its revocation, a decision of the waste disposal authority is held in suspension until the appeal is dismissed or withdrawn (s10(2)). However, there are exclusions to this provision (sub-s(3)) which arise where:

    (1) the notice was served in pursuance of s7 (variation and revocation) or s9(4)(b) (revocation after failure to comply with notice to comply with a condition); and
    (2) the authority includes in their notice a statement that in their opinion it is necessary for the purpose of preventing pollution of water or danger to public health that the suspension of revocation provisions should not apply.

If this notice has been included then the waste disposal licence remains varied or revoked until the decision on appeal of the Secretary of State is made. However, there is an interim provision (s10(3)) which allows the holder or former holder of the relevant licence to apply to the Secretary of State to determine that the authority has acted unreasonably in including such a statement in their notice. If the Secretary of State agrees with that assertion the suspension is lifted at the end of the day upon which the Secretary of State's determination is made and until such time as the appeal itself is determined. Furthermore the holder or former holder of the licence is entitled to recover compensation from the authority in respect of any loss suffered by him in consequence of the statement. Disputes as to compensation are required to be determined by arbitration (see Arbitration Act 1950).

Local authority site approvals

Section 11 applies where the land accommodating the disposal operation is occupied by the disposal authority itself. Special procedures then apply to protect the interests of, *inter alia*, the National Rivers Authority and the public.

Special wastes

By s17 powers are taken by the Secretary of State to impose a special regime of control in respect of dangerous or intractable waste. In pursuance of this section the Secretary of State has made the Control of Pollution (Special Waste) Regulations 1980 (SI 1980 No 1709). These regulations deal with a special system of control in respect of waste which is dangerous or difficult to dispose of. Special wastes are defined in the regulations. These regulations control the duties of carriers and disposers, importers and exporters and impose a system of ancillary consignment notes which must accompany the waste from its place of production to point of disposal.

Environmental Protection Act 1990

Part II of this Act will be brought into force on a date to be announced. The intention is that the whole of the Control of Pollution Act 1974 Pt I will be repealed and replaced by the 1990 Act. As such, the replacement will represent a major overhaul of the powers and responsibilities of the 1974 Act.

There is intended to be little change in administration. The same authorities which are waste disposal authorities under the 1974 Act will largely be waste regulation authorities within the meaning of the 1990 Act (s30(1)). Special arrangements exist in Greater London and the metropolitan counties. However, the powers of the authorities to themselves dispose of waste are brought to an end. The Act establishes a regime whereby the authorities in question will be required to form or participate in forming waste disposal companies ie separate entities from the local authority from which they derive; alternatively, they may use the private sector or a combination of both.

Unauthorised depositing, treatment or disposal of waste (s33)

Except in relation to household waste on a domestic property and other special cases prescribed by the Secretary of State for the Environment, it will be an offence to:

(a) deposit controlled waste or knowingly cause or knowingly permit controlled waste to be deposited in or on any land unless a waste management licence authorising the deposit is in force and the conditions of that licence are complied with.

(b) treat, keep or dispose of controlled waste or knowingly cause or knowingly permit controlled waste to be treated, kept or disposed of in or on any land or by means of any mobile plant except in accordance with a waste management licence.

(c) treat, keep or dispose of controlled waste in a manner likely to cause pollution of the environment or harm to human health. The environment is defined in s29 as including land, water and the air and 'pollution of the environment' is defined as resulting from the release or escape into any environmental medium from the land on which the waste is treated, kept or deposited or the fixed plant by means of which waste is treated, kept or disposed of. The definitions also relate to mobile plant in the same way as applies to fixed plant. 'Harm' is defined in s29(5) as meaning harm to the health of living organisms or other interference with the ecological systems of which they form part and in the case of man includes offence to any of his senses or harm to his property.

Generally speaking, the definitions of 'waste' and 'controlled waste' are similar to those applying to the 1974 Act but the 1990 Act contains more detail (see s75).

Duty of care as respects waste

Not only is there a prohibition on unauthorised depositing, keeping, treatment or disposal of waste (s33) but a new duty of care is imposed by s34. The duty of care extends to any person who imports, produces, carries, keeps, treats or disposes of controlled waste or, as a broker, has control of such waste. The duty extends to the taking of all such measures as are applicable to that person in his capacity as are reasonable in the circumstances:

(a) to prevent any contravention by any other person of s33;
(b) to prevent the escape of waste from his control or that of any other person; and
(c) on the transfer of waste, to secure that this is only to an authorised person or to a person authorised for transport purposes and that there is transferred a written description of the waste to enable such other persons to avoid contravention of s33 and to comply with the duty to prevent the escape of waste (see above).

Generally speaking the duty of care responsibilities do not apply to domestic property and the household waste produced there.

Authorised persons

These are defined in s34(3) as comprising:

(a) a waste collection authority.
(b) the holder of a waste management licence under s35 or under s5 of the 1974 Act;
(c) a person authorised by s34(3);
(d) a registered carrier of controlled waste under Control of Pollution (Amendment) Act 1989 or a person exempted by regulations under s1(3) of that Act (see below).

Code of practice

It is the intention of the Secretary of State to publish a code of practice giving practical guidance on the discharge of duty of care. Any code of practice will be admissible in evidence, particularly in deciding whether an offence has been committed under s34(6) (see below).

The Department of the Environment intend that the duty of care requirements of the Act will be brought into force from April 1992.

Offences

Sections 33 and 34 contain provisions relating to offences as follows:

By s33(6) the unauthorised depositing, treatment or disposal of waste without a licence or in contravention of a condition of that licence is an offence, although certain defences are available under sub-s(7). Proceedings may be brought for a summary conviction or on indictment, the penalties being greater in the second case. In relation to special waste (ie certain dangerous or intractable waste – see s62) penalties on conviction on an indictment extend to two years imprisonment.

A failure to comply with the duty of care provisions of s34 can also attract penalties on conviction either summarily or on indictment (s34(6)).

Special waste

The Secretary of State has taken powers under s62 to provide by regulations a special regime of control in respect of special waste.

Non-controlled waste

Section 63 contains powers for the Secretary of State to bring under control certain waste deriving from the agricultural and mines and quarries industries.

Publicity

The Environmental Protection Act 1990 includes new duties on waste regulation authorities to maintain registers containing a range of public information. This will particularly relate to information about:

    (a) current or recent licences;
    (b) current or recent applications for licences;
    (c) applications and notices relating to the modification of licences, notices relating to the revocation or suspension of licences or imposing requirements on holders;
    (d) appeals;
    (e) certificates of completion (see page 84);
    (f) convictions;
    (g) other matters relevant to the responsibilities of holders and

the authority. The form of the register and its contents will be prescribed by regulations made by the Secretary of State.

Exclusions from a register

By s65 certain information may be excluded from a register with the sanction of the Secretary of State if it would be contrary to the interests of national security. The Secretary of State has taken powers to secure the exclusion of other information and s66 allows certain confidential information of a commercial nature to be excluded under certain circumstances. However, there are restrictions on the extent to which commercial information may be excluded.

Imminent danger of serious pollution

The Act provides for action to be taken by inspectors either appointed by the Secretary of State or by the waste regulations authority. By s70 an inspector has power to enter on any premises where he has reasonable cause to believe that an article or substance is a cause of imminent danger of serious pollution of the environment or serious harm to human health. There are powers to seize and to render harmless. There are also provisions requiring samples to be given to a responsible person at the premises and for the inspector to be responsible for a written report of the circumstances. Obstruction of an inspector is an offence dealt with either summarily or on indictment.

Control of Pollution (Amendment) Act 1989

This Act, although not yet fully in force, is expected to take effect contemporaneously with Part II of the 1990 Act. It is an Act which attempts to render much more difficult the carriage of waste and the subsequent disposal of that waste in a manner falling far short of legal requirements. Following a number of unhappy examples which occurred particularly in the 1980s, including dangerous fly-tipping, Parliament decided (on a private members measure) that additional controls were necessary.

Transport in controlled waste without registering

Section 1 of the Act will make it an offence for any person, not a registered carrier of controlled waste and in the course of business or otherwise with a view to profit, to transport any controlled waste to and from any place in Great Britain. There are certain limited exceptions, which may be extended by the Secretary of State by regulations.

Registration

The Controlled Waste (Registration of Carriers and Seizure of Vehicles) Regulations 1991 SI 1991 No 1624 require registration of persons with the waste regulation authority as carriers of controlled waste. Such registers will be available to the public and will include information about applications and certain other details.

Carriers of waste will require a registration certificate, a copy of which will need to be kept on each vehicle and must be produced to an officer of the local authority or to the police. Registrations may be refused or revoked in circumstances where the applicant, or holder, or anyone associated with him has been convicted of a relevant offence or is regarded by the authority as undesirable. Appeals against refusal of registration, etc. are provided by s4 of the Act.

It is to be noted that in cases of an offence a warrant may be granted for the seizure of any vehicle involved in illegal waste disposal.

4 Hazardous substances

INTRODUCTION

This chapter deals with hazardous substances. This is a diverse subject, treated as such by the legislature. There is a wide variety of statutes dealing either wholly or in part with activities giving rise to hazardous substances and a regime of control for circumstances where escape and serious emergency might occur. This chapter does not deal with radioactive substances, a special subject which is not appropriate for a book of this type. Furthermore, a certain amount of the legislation has application mainly in the context of health and safety at work and has only tangential relevance to environmental conditions outside the place of work. However, certain parts of the Health and Safety at Work etc Act 1974 relate both to workplace and external environments and are dealt with in the following notes, by reference to appropriate subsidiary legislation.

FOOD AND ENVIRONMENT PROTECTION ACT 1985

Part 1 of this Act relates to the contamination of food and entitles the appropriate minister (usually the Minister of Agriculture, Fisheries and Food) to make emergency orders where there has been or may have been an escape of substances:

(a) likely to create a hazard to human health through human consumption of food; or
(b) which are or may be in the future derived from anything which is or may become unsuitable for human consumption. A range of activities that may be prohibited in a specific area is set out in Sch1 to the Act.

47

Practitioners will be familiar with the procedures which were last used extensively as a consequence of the Chernobyl incident in 1986. More recently, contamination of feeding stuffs orders were made in 1990 when there were fears of contamination of imported animal feed by the escape of lead.

Section 1 of the Act makes it an offence to contravene an emergency prohibition but certain actions may be approved by the appropriate minister under s2 (see Chapter 10). Provided that the required consent has been given and that any conditions have been complied with then no offence is committed under s1.

The section also provides the appropriate ministers with power to give directions to prevent human consumption of food where it is believed to be unsuitable and there is a blanket power to do all that is necessary for expedience. A failure to comply with a direction or the act of causing or permitting another to do is an offence (s2).

Investigating and enforcement officers are provided with wide powers by s3 and 4 of the Act.

Pesticides

The Food and Environment Protection Act 1985, Pt II, also gives to the enforcing ministers powers to make regulations:

(a) to protect the health of human beings, creatures and plants;
(b) to safeguard the environment;
(c) to secure safe, efficient and humane methods of controlling pests; and
(d) to provide information on these subjects. These powers are effected by regulations. The powers include rights to impose prohibitions, approve pesticides for specified uses, require consent to anything contrary to a prohibition and to generally review. Powers of seizure are also provided. For regulations made under the Act see the Control of Pesticides Regulations 1986 (SI 1986 No 1510).

Codes of practice and enforcement

Section 16 and 17 of the Act provide for codes of practice to be set up by ministers. In this regard they are advised by the Advisory Committee on Pesticides (see the Control of Pesticides (Advisory

Committee on Pesticides) (Terms of Office) Regulations 1985 (SI 1985 No 517)). Section 19 spells out the enforcement powers of inspectors giving wide powers of enforcement, entry and direction.

Penalties for offences

Section 21 of the Act specifies the penalties applicable to the offences under the Act. It is to be noted that directors and other officers of bodies corporate can be made personally liable. A general defence of due diligence is available under s22. An employee and others may have the opportunity of sheltering behind this provision.

PLANNING (HAZARDOUS SUBSTANCES) ACT 1990

Additional controls when brought into force are available by virtue of the adaptation of the town and country planning development control regime. Such regime originally derived from the insertion into the Town and Country Planning Act 1971 of a new system of control authorised by the Housing and Planning Act 1986, Pt IV. However, consolidation of the Planning Acts has now resulted in the Planning (Hazardous Substances) Act 1990. Until the 1986 Act, a system of control of operations and uses dealing with or resulting in hazardous substances was largely lacking as part of the development control system. This was because the definition in the Planning Acts of 'development' was so wide that it gave freedom so that new hazardous uses and products could often be introduced, for example to a major factory operation, without any further planning consent being required. Whilst the Health and Safety at Work etc Act 1974 controls did exist, the powers of the executive were limited so far as planning control was concerned.

The overall effect of this Act will be that the keeping of any hazardous substances on, over or under land, beyond small quantities, will require consent of the hazardous substances authority, ie usually the London boroughs, the district councils in metropolitan counties and the district planning authorities elsewhere. Regulations dealing with applications for consent and other matters will be prescribed but the procedures will be similar to those relating to planning control.

Definition of 'hazardous substance'

This is not specifically defined in the Act but lists will be prescribed by regulations.

Deemed consent (s11)

Transitional provisions will apply in those circumstances where hazardous substances have been present on the site for 12 months before the Act comes into force. A claim for a deemed consent must be made within a period of six months for commencement date.

ENVIRONMENTAL PROTECTION ACT 1990

There are two parts to this Act which have a relevance to hazardous substances and the like.

Genetically modified organisms

A new system of control is established by Pt VI of the Act, specified by s106 as having the purpose of preventing or minimising any damage to the environment which may arise from the escape or release from human control of genetically modified organisms. An 'organism' is defined in the section to mean any acellular, unicellular or multi-cellular entity (in any form) other than humans or human embryos. Unless the context otherwise requires the term also includes any article or substance consisting of or including biological matters. That term is also defined in the section.

An organism is 'genetically modified' if any of the genes or other genetic material in the organism have been modified by means of an artificial technique (to be prescribed) or are inherited or otherwise derived through any number of replications from genes or other genetic material (from any sources) which was so modified.

Damage to the environment

Section 107 specifies that damage to the environment (ie land, air, water or any of those media) is caused by the presence in the environment of genetically modified organisms which have (or of a single such organism which has) escaped or been released from a person's control and are capable of causing harm to the living organisms supported by the environment. A specification of the capability of causing harm is also provided in s107.

General controls

Section 108 *et seq* describes the powers of control available to the Secretary of State for the Environment which he will exercise by regulations. In general, there is a prohibition against importing or acquiring, releasing or marketing any genetically modified organisms without a risk assessment and notice to the Secretary of State. A registration and consent system is intended to be established by the Act.

Section 109 indicates general duties of a person relating to import-ation, acquisition, keeping, release or marketing of organisms.

Enforcement

Powers of enforcement exist in s110 (prohibition notices) and ss111–112 which relate to the requirements and procedures for consents (see Chapter 10).

Offences

A wide range of offences is set out in s118, mainly relating to failure to comply with the above procedures. It is noteworthy that by s119 the onus of proof in certain circumstances is shifted to the accused, particularly in regard to the techniques used to comply with consent obligations and monitoring.

Publicity

By s112 the Secretary of State is required to maintain a register giving a range of information concerning notices, directions, prohibition notices, applications for consent etc. Information may be excluded in certain circumstances on grounds of national security, potential damage to the environment or (subject to certain conditions) commercial confidentiality.

ENVIRONMENTAL PROTECTION ACT 1990 PT VIII

The 'miscellaneous' part of the 1990 Act contains various powers available to the Secretary of State to deal with hazardous and similar substances. These include:

(a) Power to prohibit or restrict importation, use, supply or storage of injurious substances or articles. The power permits the Secretary of State to impose prohibitions and restrictions to prevent pollution of the environment or harm to human health or the health of animals or plants. Contravention results in penalties including imprisonment and fine (s140).

(b) The Secretary of State may also make regulations enabling him to obtain information about potentially hazardous substances (s142). The specified purpose which is the basis for the demand for information is the potential for causing pollution of the environment or harm to human health.

Contaminated land

Section 143 of the 1990 Act enables the Secretary of State to establish by regulations registers of contaminated land. These regulations will specify the relevant contaminated uses of land, the form of the registers and the particulars to be included and such other matters as appear to him to be appropriate. Maintenance of the register is the responsibility of the local authority (in Greater London, the London Borough Council or the Common Council of the City of London, in England and Wales the district council). The local authority is required to ensure that the register is open to inspection by members of the public free of charge at all reasonable hours. Copies of entries in the register may be obtained on payment of reasonable charges.

5 Noise

INTRODUCTION

Until the Noise Abatement Act 1960 the control of noise largely rested upon the nuisance provisions of the Public Health Act 1936. Otherwise, control was exercised, albeit uneasily, under the town and country planning system. The incidence of complaints of noise has been steadily increasing over the past 20 years or so and this despite an overhaul of the legislation set out in the Control of Pollution Act 1974. This remains the significant statutory provision and the Environmental Protection Act 1990 has not materially modified this. However, the 1990 Act Part III is now the main provision relating to statutory nuisance procedures.

Legislation dealing with specific circumstances may be found in the Civil Aviation Act 1982 (nuisance by aircraft) and the Motor Cycle Noise Act 1987 (which limits the supply of certain exhaust systems). A wide variety of regulations relating eg to noise insulation grants for property in the hinterland of major airports, codes of practice for ice cream van chimes, burglar alarms, model aircraft etc should be noted.

CONTROL OF POLLUTION ACT 1974

Duties of local authorities

Section 57 of the Act is specific in that periodical inspections by local authorities are required to be made to decide upon the exercise of powers concerning noise abatement zones (see below).

Control of noise on construction sites

Noise from construction sites represents a major cause of complaint to

53

local authorities and others. Sections 60 and 61, therefore, present a remedy. Under s60, the local authority may serve a notice specifying how the works are to be carried out. The notice may specify which plant and machinery is to be used or not used, the hours to be worked and the level of noise. They are required to take into account any relevant codes of practice established under s71 – see the Control of Noise (Code of Practice for Construction and Open Sites) Order 1984 (SI 1984 No. 1992) and the Control of Noise (Code of Practice for Construction and Open Sites) Order 1987 (SI 1987 No. 1730). They are also required to take into account the need to secure that the best practicable means are employed to minimise noise (sub-s(4)).

Service of notice

This is served on the person who appears to the local authority to be carrying out or about to carry out the works and other persons responsible for or having control over or carrying out the works. An appeal is available to the magistrates' court within 21 days of the service of the notice but, subject to that, failure to comply with the notice results in an offence.

Prior consent for work on construction sites

It is open to any person operating a construction site to take pro-active steps to secure a local authority consent and this is dealt with under s61. By sub-s(3) an application is required to contain particulars of the works, the method by which they are to be carried out and the steps proposed to be taken to minimise noise resulting from those works. A consent in response to the notice (for which no form is prescribed) may be issued by the local authority either with or without conditions and a timetable. The effect of the consent is to avoid any action which the local authority may take under s60 but it should be noted that it does not exempt the successful applicant from the consequences of s59 (summary proceedings by occupier of premises). A refusal of consent may be the subject of an appeal to the magistrates' court (sub-s(7)).

Noise abatement zones

Continuing the theme of pro-activity by local authorities in regard to

noise, s63 of the Act provides for the designation by a local authority
of all or any part of its area as a noise abatement zone. The procedure
for doing this is set out in Sch 1 to the Act but it has been revised by
Sch 2 to the Local Government Planning and Land Act 1980.

Consequence of noise abatement zone – noise level registers

Once the noise abatement order is made, it triggers responsibilities on
the local authority to take steps, as soon as practicable, to record the
level of noise emanating from premises of a class prescribed in the
order. All measurements will need to be recorded in a noise level
register with copies of entries served on relevant owners and occupiers. Such owners and occupiers may appeal to the Secretary of
State against the record within 28 days if they wish to object to its
accuracy. This is often important because otherwise the validity or
accuracy of any entry in the register is not to be questioned in any
proceedings under this part of the Act. The register is open to public
inspection.

Effect of registration

The effect of registration is that the recorded level of noise may not be
exceeded except with consent of the local authority. Applications for
consent are dealt with under s65.

Reduction of noise levels

A second consequence of the establishment of a noise abatement zone
is that it is open to the local authority to take steps to reduce noise
deriving from any premises. They will do this under s66 by serving a
notice on the person responsible requiring reduction in the level of
noise, the prevention of any subsequent increase without consent and
the taking of such steps as specified in the notice to achieve these
purposes. The notice is known by the terms of the section as a 'noise
reduction notice' which will set a time limit being not less than six
months from the date of the service of the notice within which the
noise level is to be reduced. Particulars of the noise reduction notice
are to be recorded in the noise level register (see above). There is a
right of appeal against the noise reduction notice, to the magistrates'
court within three months of the date of service.

Practitioners should give consideration to the Control of Noise (Measurement and Registers) Regulations 1976 (SI 1976 No. 37).

Appeals

It will have been noted that there are various rights of appeal deriving from provisions in the 1974 Act. The procedure for dealing with appeals is set out in the Control of Noise (Appeals) Regulations 1975 (SI 1975 No. 2116).

PART II

Applications for approvals
and other procedures

6 Statutory Nuisances

Hitherto in this volume the statutory codes have been dealt with by reference to separate aspects of the environment. However, the most commonly encountered procedures transcend those boundaries and, as we shall see, cover a whole range of different environmental offences. The law relating to statutory nuisance is now embodied in the Environmental Protection Act 1990 Part III. This offers to the local public health authority a procedure for dealing with nuisance if they are satisfied that the statutory nuisance exists or is likely to occur or recur. In brief, the action to be taken includes the service of an abatement notice, in respect of which the person served may appeal to the magistrates court within 21 days. The court has power to support, modify or dismiss the abatement notice. Assuming its confirmation, then failure to comply with it is an offence and at this stage the local public health authority may themselves take the necessary action and recover their costs. Additionally an offence is created by the failure to comply with an abatement notice which can result in liability on summary conviction to a fine not exceeding £20,000.

The provisions of the Environmental Protection Act 1990 section 79 to 85 came into force on 1 January 1991. There are regulations relating to appeals ie the Statutory Nuisance (Appeals) Regulations 1990 SI 1990 No 2276.

WHAT IS A STATUTORY NUISANCE?

In general terms 'statutory nuisance' is defined by section 79 of the 1990 Act as:

    (a) Any premises in such a state as to be prejudicial to health or a nuisance.

(b) Smoke emitted from premises so as to be prejudicial to health or a nuisance.

(c) Fumes or gas emitted from premises so as to be prejudicial to health or a nuisance.

(d) Any dust, steam, smell or other effluvia arising on industrial, trade or business premises and being prejudicial to health or a nuisance.

(e) Any accumulation or deposit which is prejudicial to health or a nuisance,

(f) Any animal kept in such a place or manner as to be prejudicial to health or a nuisance,

(g) Noise emitted from premises so as to be prejudicial to health or a nuisance,

(h) Any other matter declared by any enactment to be a statutory nuisance.

There have been a large number of cases in which the definition of 'statutory nuisance' has been considered of which the following may be noted.

Pontardawe RDC v *Moore-Gwyn* (1929) 1 Ch 656 (premises)
National Coal Board v *Thorn* (1976) 1 WLR 543 (nuisance)
Coventry City Council v *Cartwright* (1975) 1 WLR 845 (prejudicial to health)
Malton Board of Health v *Malton Manure Co* (1879) 4 Ex D 302 (effluvia)
Wivenhoe Port v *Colchester Borough Council* (1985) JPL 175 (dust)
R v *Walden-Jones ex parte Coton* (1963) Crim LR 839 (animals)
Galer v *Morrissey* (1955) 1 All ER 380 (noisy animal)
Tower Hamlets LBC v *Manzoni and Walder* (1984) JP 123 (noise)

Summary Proceedings

The action to be taken by the local authority where they believe that a statutory nuisance arises or might occur or recur is to serve an abatement notice which can require the nuisance to be stopped or reduced or which can seek the prevention of its occurrence or recurrence. The notice may also require the execution of works and the taking of other steps to achieve these purposes. The notice is required to set time limits for the taking of any necessary action. It is usually to be served on the person responsible for the nuisance but where that person cannot be found then the notice goes to the owner or occupier of the premises. In cases where the complaint is of a defect of structural character then the owner of the premises in question is to receive the notice.

Certain proceedings may not be started by the local authority without the consent of the Secretary of State. Smoke, fumes, gas, dust, steam, smell or other effluvia emitted from premises the subject of Part I of the Alkali Etc. Works Regulations 1906 are the responsibility of Her Majesty's Inspectorate of Pollution and the Health and Safety Commission. The intention is to avoid duplication of controls.

A special defence is available in cases of abatement notices served in respect of industry, trade or business premises where the nuisance relates to paragraphs a, d, e, f and g of section 79 (above). The defence is also available in respect of paragraph b but not where the nuisance constitutes smoke emitted from a chimney.

Appeals

By section 80 anyone receiving a notice may appeal to the magistrates court within 21 days of the date on which he was served with the notice. If he does not do this and does not comply with the notice, he is liable to prosecution.

Rights to appeal are established by section 80(3) and the procedures for this, by the Statutory Nuisance (Appeals) Regulations 1990 SI 1990 No 2276. There is a substantial list of grounds of appeal of which the following is a summary.

(a) That the abatement notice is not justified by section 80 of the 1990 Act.

(b) That there has been some informality, defect or error with the notice.

(c) The authority have refused unreasonably to accept compliance with alternative requirements or the requirements of the abatement notice are otherwise unreasonable in character or extent, or are unnecessary.

(d) The time given by the abatement notice for compliance is not reasonably sufficient.

(e) That the best practicable means (see below) have been used to prevent or counteract the effects of the nuisance – only available in respect of the nuisances mentioned above and (so far as appeals are concerned) in relation to smoke emitted from a chimney.

(f) In the case of a nuisance relating to noise, that the requirements are more onerous than those in force as a result of notices relating to the control of noise levels, served under ss60 to 67 of the Control of Pollution Act 1974 (see Chap 5).

(g,h and i) That the abatement notice should or might have been served on some other person, besides or in addition to the appellant. In most cases under this ground the appellant is required to serve a copy of his notice of appeal on that other person.

Appeal Hearing

The magistrates court is required to either quash the abatement notice, vary it if this can be done in favour of the appellant or dismiss it. During the period of the appeal the abatement notice is suspended except in the special case where it alleges injury to health or that the nuisance is or is anticipated to be of limited duration.

Complaint by a member of the public

Whilst normally the aggrieved member of the public would complain about a nuisance to the public health authority who could be expected to take the appropriate action, an alternative option is to make use of s82 of the Act. This entitles a member of the public to make a complaint direct to the magistrtes court on the ground that he is aggrieved by the existence of a statutory nuisance. Upon being satisfied as to this, the court is required to make an order on the defendant to abate the nuisance, to prohibit recurrence and to execute any necessary works. The power to fine the defendant is also available. It is to be noted that the 'best practicable means' defence is also available here.

'Best Practicable Means'

The defence of 'best practicable means' has its roots in the Public Health Act 1936 and acknowledges the need for reasonableness in applying the requirements of the law of nuisance in the case of business premises and activities where compliance might well result in an uneconomic operation. Reduced to its basics, the concept takes account of the jobs v. environment argument.

The term 'best practicable means' is interpreted in s79(9) of the 1990 Act as follows:

(a) 'Practicable' means reasonably practicable having regard among other things to local conditions and circumstances, to the current state of technical knowledge and to the financial implications.

(b) The means to be employed include the design, installation, maintenance and manner and periods of operation of plant and machinery, and the design, construction and maintenance of buildings and structures.

(c) The test is to apply only so far as compatible with any duty imposed by law.

(d) The test is to apply only so far as compatible with safety and safe working conditions and with the exigencies of any emergency or unforeseeable circumstances.

Some guidance in the interpretation of the definition in relation to noise can be found in codes of practice which have been published under s71 of the Control of Pollution Act 1974.

It is important to appreciate that the best practicable means defence is not by any means a soft option for industry. See for example *Scholefield* v *Schunck* (1855) 19 JP 84 and *Wivenhoe Port* v *Colchester Borough Council* (1985) JPL 175.

7 Water

ABSTRACTION

Water Resources Act 1991

There are a limited number of people who may apply for a licence to abstract water. Occupation of the land adjacent to the inland water, or above the underground strata is usually required.

Inland water

An inland water is defined by s221 of the Act and in general will include a river, stream or other water-course either natural, artificial or tidal. It will also include any lake or pond, reservoir or dock. The resources, in each case, may be natural or artificial. Also included in the definition is so much of any channel, creek, bay, estuary or arm of the sea which lies within the National River Authority area. The regional office of the Authority will be in a position to define this. A person who wishes to abstract from an inland water must be the occupier of land contiguous to it or (when the licence is granted) have a right of access to that land.

Underground strata

This, too, is defined by s221 to mean largely what it says. The person entitled to abstract from underground strata is the occupier of the land where the underground strata is or where there is an excavation into underground strata the person who, when the licence has effect, has a right of access to the land above the underground strata.

Applications for licences to abstract

The procedure for applications is dealt with in the Water Resources (Licences) Regulations 1965 (SI 1965 No 534). Model forms of application are set out in Sch1 to the regulations. An application is made to the National Rivers Authority on the form which is obtainable from them. The application is required to be accompanied by a map to a scale of not less than 6 inches to 1 mile or the metric equivalent. The map needs to show every point of abstraction proposed and the land which is occupied by the applicant. In most cases the application must also show the land on which it is proposed to use the water. In circumstances where the water is to be used for different purposes then this should be distinguished on the map. Where the applicant is not the occupier then evidence must be provided that will show that access to the relevant land will be available if the licence is granted.

Notice under s37

Section 37 requires publication of notice of an application for a licence in the *London Gazette* and at least once in each of two successive weeks in local newspapers. If the licence is for abstraction from an inland water then the notice must, not later than the date on which it was first published in the local newspaper, be served on any navigation authority, harbour authority or conservancy authority responsible for that inland water at the point of proposed abstraction. The internal drainage board must also be served and any local water undertaker.

Contents of the newspaper notice

Forms of the notice are set out in Sch 2 to the 1965 regulations. Besides describing the proposals, the notices are required by s37 of the 1991 Act to name a place in the locality where a copy of the application and other submitted documents can be inspected at all reasonable hours and state that any person may make representations in writing to the NRA concerning the application before the end of the period specified in the notice, ie not less than 28 days from the date of local advertisement.

Documents required

The applicant must send to the NRA the forms of application and plans, copies of the newspapers containing the appropriate s37 notice and a declaration signed on behalf of the applicant that the notice has been published in the *London Gazette* (giving the date of publication). Where the notice has been served on any authority then details must be given in the declaration.

Application for a licence to impound or for a combined licence

Impounding of an inland water is forbidden unless a licence is granted by the National Rivers Authority and other conditions contained in s37 of the 1991 Act are met.

Procedure for application

The procedure is controlled by reg8 of the 1965 regulations and is similar to that for an abstraction licence. A map must accompany the application showing, *inter alia*, the location of the impounding works, the extent of such land to be submerged, any points of discharge.

Newspaper advertisements and notice to other authorities are similarly required as for a licence to abstract.

There are also special provisions in reg8 for a combined abstraction/impounding licence.

Succession to a licence

This is dealt with under ss49 and 50 of the 1991 Act and is mainly a formal matter of notification to the NRA.

Revocation or variation of licence

(a) ON APPLICATION BY HOLDER

This is a simple application under s51 and the Water Resources (Licences) Regulations 1965, reg9. In the case of variation, the procedures for publicity will also apply as they do for the licence applications (see above), unless the variation is limited simply to reducing the quantity of water authorised to be abstracted.

(b) BY THE NATIONAL RIVERS AUTHORITY

If the NRA decides to revoke or vary a licence they are obliged to notify the holder and give publicity similar to that above mentioned. The holder has a right to object (s53(4)) at which stage the proposals are referred to the Secretary of State who will make the decision. However, if no objection is raised then the matter may be dealt with by the NRA. In the circumstances defined by s61 of the 1991 Act compensation for revocation or variation will follow.

Appeals

An appeal against a decision of the National Rivers Authority or in default of decision may be made to the Secretary of State. There is no specified form but the appeal is required to be in writing and a copy must be served on the NRA. All this must be undertaken within 28 days from the date when any decision was notified to the appellant.

Application period

The National Rivers Authority has three months to consider applications. In default of a decision within that period or such extended period as is agreed with the applicant, he may appeal to the Secretary of State on grounds of non-determination.

The procedure for appeals is governed by regulation 12 of the 1965 regulations.

WATER POLLUTION

Public Health (Drainage of Trade Premises) Act 1937

There is a right subject to the provisions of the Act to discharge trade effluents into public sewers. A 'trade effluent' is defined by s14 to mean any liquid, either with or without particles of matter in suspension therein, which is wholly or in part produced in the course of any trade or industry carried on at trade premises and, in relation to any trade premises, means any such liquid as aforesaid which is so produced in the course of any trade or industry carried on at those premises, but does not include domestic sewage.

'Trade premises' means any premises used or intended to be used for carrying on any trade or industry.

Procedure

Trade effluent may not be discharged from any trade premises except in accordance with a written notice (called in the Act a 'trade effluent notice'). This is served on the appropriate water company for the area. There is no prescribed form but s2 of the Act specifies that the notice must contain details of the nature or composition of the trade effluent, the maximum quantity of the effluent proposed to be discharged per day and the highest rate at which discharge will take place. The notice is required to be served by the owner or occupier of the premises in question and must be served at least two months (unless any lesser period has been agreed) before the discharge actually starts.

It is open to the appropriate water company for the area to prohibit the discharge or issue a consent with or without specific conditions. The extent to which conditions may be imposed is defined in s2(3). Note that the 1937 Act needs to be read together with the Public Health Act 1936, the Public Health Act 1961 and the Control of Pollution Act 1974. Some further amendments have been effected by the Water Resources Act 1991 and there are alternative procedures in both the 1961 and 1974 Acts for dealing with discharges of trade effluents to public sewers.

Appeals

Where an owner or occupier is dissatisfied with the response of the appropriate water company for the area to his trade effluent notice he may avail himself of the right of appeal under s3 of the Act of 1937 as supplemented by s61 of the 1961 Act. No specific procedure has been laid down.

Trade effluent agreement

Section 7 of the 1937 Act provides for agreements to be made with the appropriate water company for the area. The agreement can relate to the reception and disposal by the water company of any trade effluent produced on the owner/occupier's premises and can deal with the construction by the water company of any works required for reception or disposal and payment of expenses by the owner/occupier. It should be noted that the agreement is binding only on the owner/occupier at the time when it was made and a fresh agreement would need to be negotiated on any change of ownership or occupation.

Powers to vary conditions

The water company has the power to vary conditions of any previously consented discharge of trade effluent into a public sewer. These powers arise from s60 of the Public Health Act 1961.

Extension of 1937 Act to other effluents

Section 64 of the 1961 Act gives power to the Secretary of State for the Environment to extend the definition of trade effluents to other types of effluent. The orders are local in nature and practitioners would need to confirm with the local water company whether such orders apply in the area in question.

Water Resources Act 1991 – authority for discharges

A person avoids an offence under s85 of the 1991 Act by securing and complying with either a consent under the 1991 Act or the Control of Pollution Act 1974 or a licence granted under Pt II of the Food and Environment Protection Act 1985 (discharge of substances into the sea) or any local Act or prescribed enactment. It is to be noted that the Water Resources Act 1991 also controls discharges to 'controlled waters', defined in s104 of the 1991 Act. The definition is a long one but in general terms includes the sea, rivers and water-courses, lakes and ponds, the underground aquifer and underground excavations.

Applications for consent

These are made under s88 of and Sch10 to the 1991 Act. The procedures of Sch10 require an application to be made to the National Rivers Authority who itself must publish notice of the application in local newspapers and in the *London Gazette*. A copy of the application is required to be sent by the NRA to every local authority or water undertaker where the discharge is to occur and where such discharge is into coastal waters copies are also to be served on the Secretary of

State and the Minister of Agriculture, Fisheries and Food. Publicity for the application may be avoided in circumstances where the authority proposes to give the consent applied for and considers the discharge will have 'no appreciable effect' on the receiving waters. The phrase has been considered in relation to the 1974 Act by Department of the Environment circular 17/84, 'Water and the Environment'.

8 Air pollution and integrated pollution control

CONTROL OF INDUSTRIAL AIR POLLUTION (REGISTRATION OF WORKS) REGULATIONS 1989

At time of writing these regulations represent one of the two systems for control of air pollution by major processes. The regulations envisage a requirement for application for registration. This registration is required to be made by the owner of the works in question who must supply the following particulars:

(a) the name and address of the owner of the work and, if a company registered under the Companies Act, the name, registered number and registered office of the company;

(b) the name and address of the premises where the work is situated;

(c) the identification of the works by reference to a map or plan or otherwise;

(d) the name of the relevant local authority;

(e) the date on which the application is made;

(f) a full description of the nature of the work carried on or proposed to be carried on;

(g) a description of the source, nature and amount of any noxious or offensive substance that may be emitted into the atmosphere as a result of carrying on the works;

(h) a description of the means proposed to enable the works to be carried on in accordance with the legislation;

(i) a description of the provision the applicant has proposed to make for determining the nature and amount of any noxious or offensive substance emitted into the atmosphere (monitoring).

Notice of application

The application is made to the Secretary of State for the Environment although administration is devolved to Her Majesty's Inspectorate of Pollution (HMIP). There is a requirement by reg4 of the 1989 regulations to publish within 14 days of the application in a local newspaper and in successive weeks a notice giving details of the application, an indication of the place where the application may be inspected and a statement to the effect that written representations can be made to the Secretary of State within 21 days of the first newspaper publication. A copy of the notice is required to go to the Secretary of State together with the certificate of publication. The combined effect of regs4 and 5 is that the notice of application must be advertised between 14 days and six months after the date that the application has been received by the Secretary of State.

Public access to applications

Whilst in the main all applications are available for inspection by the public there are provisions for the Secretary of State to exempt from disclosure any particulars which would prejudice unreasonably some private interest concerning a trade secret or prejudice the interests of national defence. The local authority also has obligations to keep the application available for inspection.

The register

All works required to be registered shall be recorded in a register for that purpose as controlled by reg7 of the 1989 regulations, to which the public has access. A duplicate part of the register relating to works within its area is also made available by the Secretary of State to the local authority in question.

Certificate of registration

This important document confirms that the works are registered for the purposes of the legislation and remains in force until the work to which it relates is closed for a period of 12 months or more or a new certificate is issued in replacement (reg9).

Notification of changes to works

The owner must notify changes appropriate to the certificate of registration within one month of the change taking place.

INTEGRATED POLLUTION AND AIR POLLUTION CONTROL BY LOCAL AUTHORITIES

Regulations under the Environmental Protection Act 1990

Part I of this Act will be brought into force for all new prescribed processes and this began in 1991.

There are now a number of sets of regulations which control procedures and applications for authorisations under the Integrated Pollution Control provisions of the Act. The regulations also deal with applications to local public health authorities for authorisations for those lesser polluting processes and here the control is limited to air pollution only (although other controls may apply by virtue of other legislation).

Prescribed Processes and Substances

It is first necessary to clarify whether a given process is the subject of integrated pollution control (IPC) or local authority control. This may be ascertained by reference to the Environmental Protection (Prescribed Processes and Substances) Regulations 1991 SI 1991 No 472 which has been slightly amended by the Environmental Protection (Amendment of Regulations) Regulations 1991 SI 1991 No 836. These regulations which came into force in England and Wales on 1 April 1991 set out in schedule 1 descriptions of the various processes in respect of which authorisations are required. The schedule divides processes into part A and part B. Part A lists processes the subject of IPC whilst part B describes processes which will be controlled by local authorities. See appendices A and B (post) for general lists respectively of these processes.

Once it is concluded that the process is caught by the regulations, then attention needs to be paid to the rules relating to applications.

Applications, Appeals and Registers

These matters are controlled by the Environmental Protection (Applications Appeals and Registers) Regulations 1991 SI 1991 No 507. These deal in some detail with the procedures to be followed where it is necessary to make applications for authorisation to carry on a prescribed process. It should be noted that in the initial years of the new Environmental Protection Act, an application for an authorisation will only be needed where a) there is a new process b) an existing process is substantially changed and c) where further regulations provide that specific processes, whether new or existing, require a specific authorisation.

The above regulations set out in some detail what is required. See appendix D (post) for a typical application form.

Guidance Notes

A wide range of guidance notes have been prepared and these fall into three categories.

(i)   General. Examples here are 'Integrated Pollution Control. A Practical Guide' – published by the Department of the Environment and the Welsh Office, general guidance notes for local authorities (GG1 to 5) published by the Department of the Environment, the Scottish Office and Welsh Office.

(ii)   Industry sector guides IPR 1 to 5 covering the main industrial sectors and giving general guidance on the processes and procedures.

(iii) Specific industry guidance notes. These relate to particular processes and the substances produced by the processes which are under the control of the Act.

Determination Periods

The Secretary of State has also published regulations which set down time limits for consideration of authorisation applications. These are the Environmental Protection (Authorisation of Processes) (Determination Periods) Order 1991 SI 1991 No 513. The regulations are in essence variations of the period set out in schedule 1 to the Act (usually 4 months), although by ss21 and 22 there are special arrangements in circumstances where confidentiality of parts of the applications is sought.

The timetable for implementing Integrated Pollution Control (during a period extending to the end of 1995) is set out in Appendix A to the Integrated Pollution Control practical guide referred to above.

9 Waste on land

APPLICATIONS UNDER CONTROL OF
POLLUTION ACT 1974

Applications for licences to dispose of waste are presently controlled by s5 of the Control of Pollution Act 1974. The procedure is governed by the Collection and Disposal of Waste Regulations 1988 (SI 1988 No. 819). Whilst the application must be in writing, there is no prescribed form. The application is made to the disposal authorities, most of whom have prepared their own application form. By sub-(2) a disposal authority may not issue a licence until they are satisfied that planning consent under the Town and Country Planning Act 1990 is in force for the use of the land, plant or equipment to which the licence is to relate. Once that consent is in force then the waste disposal authority may not reject the application unless the authority is satisfied that its rejection is necessary for the prevention of pollution of water or danger to public health.

By s5(4) a disposal authority proposing to issue a licence must, before it does so, consult:

(a) the National Rivers Authority;
(b) in the case of the London Waste Regulation Authority, any London waste disposal authority and any collection authority whose area includes any part of the relevant land;
(c) in all other cases, any collection authority in whose area the land in question is included.

The disposal authority's responsibility also include the duty to consider any representation received from the above-mentioned bodies within 21 days (or longer period if agreed between them). In circumstances where the National Rivers Authority requests the disposal authority not to issue the licence or disagrees with proposed conditions of the licence then either may refer the matter to the Secretary of State. The licence shall not be issued except in accordance with his decision.

Conditions of a licence

Section 6 of the Act makes provision for the conditions of any disposal licence. These conditions may relate to:

(a) the duration of the licence;
(b) the supervision by the holder of activities to which the licence relates;
(c) the kinds and qualities of waste which may be dealt with in pursuance of the licence, the methods of dealing with them and the recording of information;
(d) precautions to be taken on the land to which the licence relates;
(e) the steps to be taken to facilitate compliance with conditions of the planning permission from which the licence is based;
(f) the hours of working;
(g) any works to be carried out in connection with the land, plant or equipment to which the licence relates, before the activities authorised by the licence are begun or while they are continuing.

Register of licences

Once a licence is granted a copy of it is required by the disposal authority to be maintained in a register which is to be open to inspection by the public free of charge at all reasonable hours. Members of the public may obtain copies of entries in the register on payment of a reasonable charge.

Appeal against non-determination

An applicant may appeal against non-determination after two months have elapsed from the date when the disposal authority receives the application or such longer period as the authority and the applicant may agree in writing.

Variation of conditions and revocation of licences

Variation of conditions of an extant licence may be pursed in two alternative ways:

(1) By the disposal authority. The authority may serve a notice on the holder of the licence modifying the conditions specified to any extent, which in the opinion of the authority, is desirable and which is unlikely to require unreasonable expenditure by the licence holder.

(2) By the licence holder. The licence holder may request a modification which is secured by notice from the disposal authority confirming the modification.

Section 7 imposes an obligation on the disposal authority to make a modification of a licence in circumstances where pollution of water or danger to public health might arise or where there may be serious detriment to the amenities of the locality affected by the activities the subject of the licence. However, by s7(4) if the danger of pollution of water or to public health or to local amenity is so serious that a modification of a condition is inadequate then the duty of the authority is to revoke the licence.

Transfer and relinquishment of licences

The holder of a disposal licence may transfer such licence by giving notice to the authority indicating the date of transfer and details of the name and address of the transferee. The disposal authority has the right, within eight weeks of the notice having been received, to give counter-notice to the transferee that it declines to accept him as holder of the licence. Thereupon the licence ceases to have effect after a further period of two weeks. An appeal appears to lie under s10(1)(a).

Section 8(4) enables the holder of a disposal licence to cancel it by simple delivery to the authority which issued it and notice to that authority that he no longer requires the licence. However, it should be noted that this right will shortly be brought to an end once Part II of the Environmental Protection Act 1990 is brought into force.

APPLICATIONS UNDER THE ENVIRONMENTAL PROTECTION ACT 1990

The 1990 Act contains new powers in relation to waste management licences. These powers are contained in s35 to 44 and will replace the provisions relating to waste disposal licences contained in the Control of Pollution Act 1974. It is intended that the powers under the 1990 Act will be brought into force by regulations but no such regulations have yet been passed.

Waste management licences

The licence is granted by the Waste Regulation Authority and will authorise the treatment, keeping or disposal of controlled waste in or on specified land or the treatment or disposal by means of a specified mobile plant.

Application

An application is required to be made by:

(1) the occupier in the case of a licence relating to the treatment, keeping or disposal of waste in or on land.
(2) the operator in the case of a licence for the treatment or disposal of waste by means of a mobile plant.

The application is expected to be made by specified form and will be made to the waste regulation authority where the land is situated. However, in the case of a mobile plant licence the operator must apply to the authority where he has his principal place of business. A fee for the application will be prescribed and will be payable under s41.

No licence may be issued unless planning permission is in force or a certificate establishing the use for the purpose exists under the Town and Country Planning Act 1990.

The waste regulation authority may not reject the application unless:

(1) the applicant is not a fit and proper person (see below);
(2) rejection is necessary for the purpose of preventing pollution of the environment, harm to human health or serious detriment to the amenities of the locality.

However, the last reason (relating to amenity) is inapplicable where planning permission is in force in relation to the use to be the subject of the licence.

Consultations

The waste regulation authority may not issue a licence until it has referred the proposal to the National Rivers Authority and the Health and Safety Executive and considered any representations made by those bodies within the allowed period of 21 days starting from the day when the proposal is received by the waste disposal authority. However, s35(10) allows the authorities, apparently without reference to the applicant, to agree a longer period. The applicant's sanction is to appeal on non-determination grounds (see below).

National Rivers Authority

In those cases where a proposal has been referred to the National Rivers Authority who request that the licence be not issued or who disagree about the conditions of the proposed licence there is a provision in s36(5) for the matter to be referred to the Secretary of State. Pending his decision by way of arbitration the licence is not to be issued, and then it may only be issued in accordance with his decision.

Conditions of a licence

By s35(3) a licence is required to be granted on such terms and conditions as appear to the waste regulation authority to be appropriate. They may relate to the activities which the licence authorises and to the precautions to be taken and works to be carried out in connection with or in consequence of the activities. Conditions may require the licence-holder to carry out works or do other things even though he is not entitled to do so. Sectin 35(4) appears to contain an entirely novel provision to the effect that any person whose consent would be required *shall* grant or join in granting the holder of the licence such rights in relation to the land as will enable the holder of the licence to comply with any requirements imposed on him by the licence.

Regulations

The Secretary of State will make regulation indicating which conditions are or are not to be included in a licence.

Surrender and transfer

The 1990 Act makes changes in relation to surrender and transfer which may not be as secured except in the special circumstances of ss39 and 40 (below).

Variation

A licence may be varied under s37:

(a) On the waste regulation authority's initiative. The conditions of a licence may be modified as may be regarded as desirable by the authority provided the condition is unlikely to require unreasonable expense on the part of the holder.

(b) On the initiative of the licence-holder. The conditions may be modified to the extent requested in the application but at the discretion of the authority. A fee is payable under s41.

Modification

The waste regulation authority has further responsibilities under s37(2) to modify the conditions of a licence where this is required for the purpose of ensuring that the activities authorised do not cause pollution of the environment or harm to human health or become seriously detrimental to the amenities of the locality affected by the activities. ·Regulations made under s35(6) will control these responsibilities.

The process of modification is secured by notice served on the holder of the licence and it shall state the time when the modification is to take effect.

Revocation and suspension of licences (s38)

Revocation and suspension may be undertaken by the waste regulation authority in relation to a licence where:

(a) the holder has ceased to be a fit and proper person by reason of a conviction for a relevant offence – to be prescribed;

(b) that the continuation of the licenced activities would cause pollution of the environment, harm to human health or serious detriment to the amenities of the locality affected;

(c) that the pollution, harm or detriment cannot be avoided by modification.

Additionally, revocation to the extent specified may be exercised by the waste regulation authority where the holder has ceased to be a fit and proper person by reason of the management of the activities authorised by the licence having ceased to be in the hands of a technically competent person. For 'fit and proper person' see below p. 85.

EFFECT OF REVOCATION

Once a licence is revoked in part it shall cease to have effect to authorise the carrying on of the activities specified but it is open to the authority to retain further requirements imposed by the licence which the authority will require should continue to bind the licence-holder. This might arise where the right to continue to dispose of waste ceases but the obligation to prevent pollution caused by earlier disposals of waste may be required to continue.

SUSPENSION OF LICENCE (s38)

A licence can be suspended by a waste regulation authority where:

(a) the holder has ceased to be a fit and proper person (see below page 85) by reason of the management of the activities authorised by the licence having ceased to be in the hands of a technically competent person; or

(b) that serious pollution of the environment or serious harm to human health results from or is about to be caused by the activities to which the licence relates or some happening or threatened happening affecting those activities; and

(c) serious pollution of the environment or serious harm to human health will result if the activities or the circumstances persist.

The effect of suspension is that those activities approved by the licence, or some of them as identified by the authority, are suspended. The suspension notice may require the holder of the licence to take measures to deal with or avert the pollution or harm. Failure to comply is an offence (s38(10)).

Revocation or suspension is effected by notice served on the holder by the waste regulation authority which notice is required to state the time when any requirement is to take effect. The notice may also specify when the suspension is to cease and in what circumstances.

Surrender of licence

The 1990 Act makes significant changes to the powers of a licence-holder to surrender his licence. During the currency of the Control of Pollution Act 1974 a surrender could be affected at will and without any need for agreement by any other party.

With effect from the coming into force of s39 neither site licences under the Control of Pollution Act 1974 nor waste management licences under the 1990 Act may be surrendered except under a special regime.

WASTE MANAGEMENT LICENCES

The surrender of these licences is expected to be controlled by the conditions upon which the licence will be granted.

SITE LICENCES

Site licences under the Control of Pollution Act 1974 may only be surrendered if the authority accepts such surrender. The procedure involves the holder's making an application to the authority of the appropriate form giving information and such evidence as the Secretary of State will prescribe by regulations. A fee is payable. The regulations are likely to identify standards and criteria to be met by the licence-holder. These will deal with matters relating to pollution and health and safety of the site including the control of gas and leachate, as well as after-care. It seems likely that considerable periods of time will elapse once the completion of the main waste disposal activities are completed, before surrender can be accepted.

DUTIES OF AN AUTHORITY ON APPLICATION
FOR SURRENDER (s39)

Once the authority has received such application they are required to inspect the land and seek any further information or evidence.

Thereafter they are required by sub-s(5) to decide whether it is likely or unlikely that there will be any more pollution of the environment or harm to human health. Only when they are satisfied that pollution or harm will not happen may they accept surrender. They may only accept surrender after referring the proposal to the National Rivers Authority and considering any representations. If the National Rivers Authority requests that the surrender of licence be not accepted and a dispute with the waste regulation authority persists, then the matter may be referred to the Secretary of State for decision.

CERTIFICATE OF COMPLETION

Once surrender is accepted, the authority is required to issue to the applicant a certificate of completion stating its satisfaction. Once the certificate is issued, the licence ceases to have effect.

Transfer of licences (s40)

New controls on transfers of licences are to be brought into force by s40. The waste regulation authority will have power to ensure that transfer is only to be made to a 'fit and proper person' – see below page 85.

Appeals

Appeals are made to the Secretary of State by virtue of s43. Appeals lie on decisions (or failures to make decisions) where:

    (a) an application for licence or modification of conditions is rejected;
    (b) a licence is granted subject to conditions;
    (c) the conditions of a licence are modified;
    (d) a licence is suspended;
    (e) a licence is revoked;
    (f) an application to surrender a licence is rejected;
    (g) an application for the transfer of a licence is rejected.

The usual procedure will be for the Secretary of State to appoint an inspector (to whom he may delegate the determination). Any party to the appeal may request or the Secretary of State may decide that a hearing should be undertaken. Once the appeal is determined, the authority is required to give effect to that determination.

INTERIM PROVISIONS PENDING DETERMINATION

Pending the determination of an appeal, modification or revocation the decision in question is ineffective. However, this provision does not apply if the notice of modification or revocation includes a statement that in the opinion of the authority it is necessary for the purpose of preventing or, where that is not practicable, minimising pollution of the environment or harm to human health that the modification or revocation should not apply. However, if the Secretary of State or other person determining the appeal decides that the authority has acted unreasonably then the suspension of modification or revocation may be removed pending the final outcome of the appeal. Furthermore, the holder or former holder is then entitled to compensation from the authority for any loss suffered as a result of the unreasonable action of the authority. Compensation is settled by arbitration in the event of continuing dispute.

Meaning of 'fit and proper person'

Unless an applicant for a waste disposal licence satisfies the criteria of 'a fit and proper person' such licence may not be issued. Furthermore, any fit or proper person who ceases to be so may be required to forfeit the licence. The measurement of 'fit and proper person' is by reference to the licensed activities carried on by him and the fulfilment of the requirements of the licence.

A person is to be treated as not a fit and proper person if:

(a) he or another relevant person (see below) has been convicted of a relevant offence – to be prescribed;
(b) the management of the activities authorised by the licence is not in the hands of a technically competent person;
(c) the holder or potential holder of the licence has not made or will not make financial provision adequate to discharge the obligations arising from the licence.

It is to be noted that in relation to paragraph (a) above the treating of a convicted person as not fit and proper is at the discretion of the authority. It is the intention of the Secretary of State to issue guidance in regard to this aspect and also to prescribe offences regarded as being relevant. Regulations will also prescribe the qualifications and experience required of a technically competent person.

RELEVANT PERSON

A relevant person for the purposes of paragraph (a) above is to be treated as a person associated with the licence-holder and as having been convicted of a relevant offence if:

(a) any person has been convicted of a relevant offence in the course of his employment by the holder or carrying on business as a partner of the holder;

(b) a body corporate has been convicted of a relevant offence when the licence-holder was a director, manager, secretary or similar officer of that body;

(c) where the holder of the licence is a body corporate and a director, manager, secretary or similar officer has been convicted of a relevant offence or was in a similar position in another body when a relevant offence was committed by that body corporate.

10 Hazardous substances

FOOD AND ENVIRONMENT PROTECTION ACT 1985

Lifting of emergency order

Both the Secretary of State for the Environment and the Minister of Agriculture, Fisheries and Food have powers to lift emergency orders in any way they consider appropriate and subject to any conditions. The Act has not laid down procedures for applications other than to make provision for them under s2(1). Since, in the particular circumstances of an emergency, investigating and enforcement officers will have been empowered to take action, to the extent set out in s3 of the Act, it is clear that an informal and subsequently formal approach to the officers would be the correct course of action.

Pesticides

See Chapter 4 for a general statement of the implications of Pt II of the Food and Environment Protection Act 1985 as it applies to pesticides.

CONTROL OF PESTICIDES REGULATIONS 1986

These regulations provide, *inter alia*, the mechanisms whereby approvals can be granted for the use, supply and storage of pesticides. Approval can be full or provisional under reg5.

By reg6 consent to the advertisement of pesticides as well as to the sale, supply, storage and use of them may be given, again subject to conditions. The schedules to the regulations set out basic conditions but further ones may be added. Schedule 4 deals specifically to conditions relating to the application of pesticides from an aircraft.

PLANNING (HAZARDOUS SUBSTANCES) ACT 1990

Consent under the 1990 Act is dealt with in s6 *et seq*. Applications for consent are made to the hazardous substances authority (see Chapter 4). There is an obligation to consult with the Health and Safety Executive. The Act provides for the making of regulations by the Secretary of State setting out the procedures for applications for consents but to date, these regulations have not been promoted. Section 7 of the 1990 Act contemplates that an application will be required to be advertised and that other publicity will ensue. There is a close relationship with the procedures relating to the making of an application for planning permission under the Town and Country Planning Act 1990.

ENVIRONMENTAL PROTECTION ACT 1990 – GENETICALLY MODIFIED ORGANISMS

Consents to the importation, acquisition, release or marketing of any genetically modified organisms will be required by s111 of the Act. The section indicates that an application for a consent must contain such information and be made and advertised in such manner as may be prescribed. To date no regulation have been made. A fee will be charged in accordance with s113. There will be a requirement for notice of application to be given to prescribed persons. Section 112 makes provision for the limitations and conditions that may be imposed by the Secretary of State on any consent.

PART III

Some notes on common law and other liabilities and remedies

INTRODUCTION

For the most part the control of pollution and the maintenance of environmental protection is based upon a system of statute law, that is a succession of statutory requirements. Responsibility for enforcement rests with bodies which are creations of central or local government. However, increasingly in recent times policing bodies are being established placed more remotely from ministerial control. The most obvious example of this is the National Rivers Authority established by the Water Act 1989 and there are plans to transform Her Majesty's Inspectorate of Pollution to 'agency status'.

Thus an individual's main route of remedy is likely to be by complaint to the responsible authority, be it National Rivers Authority, Her Majesty's Inspectorate of Pollution or local government officer. The procedures set out in Parts I and II of this volume represent the most straightforward and possibly the cheapest remedy. Indeed, proceedings ultimately resulting in action by the courts have tended to exclude the common man as primary participant. Frequently there was essentially no opportunity to proceed for breach of statutory responsibility against a polluter otherwise than via the route described above.

CIVIL PROCEDURES

However, this whole raft of formal criminal procedure should not obscure the fact that civil remedies exist in common law and increasingly are enshrined in the more modern legislation. Such legislation is reflecting greater public demand to be included in the whole

process of value judgments about pollution control. Both the Water
Resources Act 1991 and the Environmental Protection Act 1990 have
enlarged the responsibilities of industrial processors and other holders
of authorisations to reveal, subject to certain protections, a considerable amount of detail about their activities and their environmental
performance. Registers of consents, the results of monitoring and
other information will now be readily available for inspection by
members of the public who will have a right to take detailed particulars. Furthermore, restrictions on independent action for criminal
sanctions against polluters are being gradually withdrawn, to the
extent that 'class' actions, eg proceedings taken by bodies formed by
persons with closely related views, such as Friends of the Earth or
Greenpeace, may be relatively common in the future.

LIABILITIES UNDER COMMON LAW

It would be inappropriate in a volume of this type to examine in detail
the law of trespass, nuisance or negligence which will be to the
forefront in any practitioner's consideration of the remedies open to a
client. Suffice it to say that it would be obvious to a practitioner that
where there is some interference from an external source with the
beneficial use of premises occupied by the plaintiff or some physical
injury to his premises or his property, or to himself, then an action in
tort will lie. It is also obvious that the rule in *Rylands* v *Fletcher* (1868)
LR 3 HL 330 will have application in many cases.

REMEDIES AT COMMON LAW

By the same token, remedies will be available to a plaintiff along the
lines of those available to him in any action for trespass, nuisance and/
or negligence. Such remedies will include the right to an injunction
and/or damages. It may also include, where he wishes to proceed
against a statutory authority, an 'administrative' remedy such as
mandamus or certiorari.

There now follows a brief examination of the civil liability and
remedy scene by reference to individual codes.

It is a defence to a common law action in nuisance that statutory
authority exists. However, that authority must be certain insofar as it

authorises the commission of a nuisance (*Allen* v *Gulf Oil Refining Limited* [1981] AC 101). The source of much guidance in regard to the law of nuisance by pollution of the atmosphere is the case of *Sturges* v *Bridgman* (1879) 11 Ch D 852. The standard of air pollution control by process operators will vary depending on the circumstances, in particular the neighbourhood and the ambient air quality. The following cases serve to clarify the extent to which the courts will go in dealing with nuisance claims and the awards of damage therefor.

Walter v *Selfe* (1852) 19 LTOS 308 (smoke).
Halsey v *Esso Petroleum Co Ltd* [1961] 2 All ER 145 (noxious smells).
West v *Bristol Tramways* [1908] 2 KB 14 (fumes).

The tort of negligence may be a relevant basis for a claim in certain circumstances (*Tutton* v *A D Walker Ltd* [1985] 3 All ER 757 and *Tysoe* v *Davies* [1984] RTR 88).

Action based upon statutory liability

The Environmental Protection Act 1990 (when fully in force) will in Pt I provide a strong basis for actions in negligence, in those cases where failure to comply with the statutory requirements is proved. Practitioners will be readily assisted by the publicity requirements of the Act – see s20 to 22 (public registers). Again, the correct basis of approach for a potential plaintiff is to seek relief under the law of nuisance. Matter escaping from a defendant's land is likely to give rise to an action in nuisance, possibly by virtue of the rule in *Rylands* v *Fletcher* (1868 LR 3HL 330). Both the common law and the rule may be particularly appropriate to those cases where noxious waste material has been deposited on a defendant's land, thereby causing offensive smells or other wind-borne or water-borne deterioration of the plaintiff's property. An action in damages might lie together in certain circumstances with the right to an injunction. See also *Leakey* v *National Trust* [1980] 1 All ER 17; *Smith* v *Great Western Railway* (1926) 42 TLR 391.

General note on common law remedies for individuals

The plaintiff would normally seek a remedy in nuisance by action for damages and an injunction will apply, particularly in those cases where a nuisance is likely to happen again. The Attorney-General may be prevailed upon to take proceedings for an injunction to prevent recurrence of public nuisance but a prior requirement would be that a large number of potential plaintiffs must be affected – see *Attorney-General* v *PYA Quarries Ltd* [1957] 2 QB 169.

Practitioners should also take into account *Gouriet* v *Union of Post Office Workers* [1978] AC 435. This House of Lords case established that an action for an injunction to restrain an anticipated breach would only be available to a private person in circumstances where special harm or damage to some private right was proved.

Attention is also drawn to the right of private persons to bring summary proceedings for statutory nuisance under s82 of the Environmental Protection Act 1990 and, in regard to litter, similar provisions in s91.

WATER POLLUTION

A riparian owner has a common law right to receive water in any stream or river, on or adjacent to his property, without harm to its natural condition. No proof of damage is required where harm arises, eg to livestock or other consumers (see *Young* v *Bankier Distillery Ltd* [1893] AC 691.) The pollution of underground water will also be actionable in common law, for example by the dumping of waste by the defendant on adjacent land which then pollutes underground resources flowing on to the plaintiff's land.

It would appear that a statutory right to pollute, eg by ss88 and 89 of the Water Resources Act 1991, is no defence to civil proceedings.

RESTRICTION ON RIGHT TO PROSECUTE

Under the Public Health Act 1936, s298, there exists a restriction on any right to prosecute without the written consent of the Attorney-General. For such consent to be granted the applicant must be the party aggrieved, ie have a genuine grievance, or the local authority who have the enforcement powers.

CONTROL OF POLLUTION ACT 1974, s88

This section provides for civil liability for contravention of s3(3), to the extent that where any damage is caused by poisonous, noxious or polluting waste deposited on land then in so far as an offence has been created under s(3) the defendant is also liable specifically in civil law. The section overcomes the difficulty which would otherwise arise from s105 of the Act which restricts the extent to which an offence under the 1974 Act can be actionable as a civil remedy.

WATER ABSTRACTION

It is only necessary to say here that an unlawful interference with the supply of surface or underground water to the extent that a plaintiff's right to abstract is detrimentally affected provides a civil action in tort against the person responsible. This is an extremely well documented branch of the law of tort and practitioners are referred to standard textbooks on the subject.

RIGHT OF ACTION AGAINST NATIONAL RIVERS AUTHORITY

The Water Resources Act 1991 contains a useful provision in circumstances where a licensed abstractor of water has suffered as a result of the breach of the duty imposed by s39 of the Act. Subject to certain conditions and restrictions there is a right of action against the National Rivers Authority under s60 of the 1991 Act where the NRA are in breach of the duty to protect the right of an abstractor who has been granted a licence and who seeks to abstract in accordance with his licence and the conditions imposed. If the National Rivers Authority have taken any action which it can be established derogates from a previous protected right then the authority is in breach of duty and may be proceeded against in respect of that breach. Circumstances such as this are most likely to arise where the authority has granted a second or subsequent abstraction right which interferes with the earlier authorisation.

STATUTORY PROVISION FOR CIVIL LIABILITY

In some circumstances the statute will modify normal civil liability rules. An example of this is in s70 of the Water Resources Act 1991. Except insofar as the Act provides expressly, restrictions on abstraction impounding and the construction of wells or boreholes are not to be construed (i) as providing any right of action in any civil proceedings or (ii) derogating from any right of action or other remedy (whether civil or criminal) in proceedings instituted otherwise under this part of the Act.

INFORMATION/REGISTERS

There is an obligation on the National Rivers Authority to keep registers of information concerning applications for grant, revocation or variation of abstraction licences and other information. Such registers are available for public inspection (Water Resources Act 1991, ss189–191.

There are a number of provisions in the Environmental Protection Act 1990 whereby public registers are to be kept: These include s20 (Part 1 authorisations), s64 (waste on land), s95 (litter), s122 (genetically modified organisms), s143 (contaminated land).

APPENDIX A

General list of IPC processes intended to be the subject of central (HMIP) control

Gasification
Carbonisation
Combustion
Petroleum

Incineration
Chemical recovery
Chemical waste treatment
Waste-derived fuel

Cement
Asbestos
Fibre
Glass
Ceramic

Petrochemical
Organic chemical
Chemical pesticide
Pharmaceutical

Mineral acid
Halogen
Chemical fertiliser
Bulk chemical storage

Inorganic chemical

Iron and steel
Smelting

Non-ferrous

Paper pulp
Di-isocyanate
Tar and bitumen
Uranium
Coating
Printing ink and coating
Timber
Animal and plant treatment

NB This is intended to be a general list and readers are advised to examine in detail the full definitions of the processes to be prescribed for IPC control.

APPENDIX B

General list of processes the subject of local authority air pollution controls

1.3 Combustion

    a. Boiler 20–50 MW
    b. Gas turbine 20–50 MW
    c. Compression engine
    d. Waste oil <0.4MW
    e. WDF
    f. Tyres
    g. Straw
    h. Wood
    i. Poultry litter
    j. Waste oil 0.4–3MW

2.1 Iron and Steel

    a. Cupolas (Hot and Cold)
    b. Electrical & rotary
    c. Foundry operations

2.2 Non-ferrous metals

    a. Aluminium
    b. Copper/brass
    c. Zinc
    d. Scrap
    e. Galvanizing
    f. Foundry operations
    g. Other non-ferrous
    h. Metal decontamination

3.1 Cement and lime

    a. Cement
    b. Lime

3.2 Asbestos

3.4 Mineral

    a. Coal
    b. Crushing/quarrying
    c. Roadstone
    d. Plaster
    e. Sand drying
    f. China clay
    g. Clay drying
    h. Perlite
    i. Vermiculite
    j. Sintered aggregates
    k. Others

3.5 Glass

    a. Glass manufacture
    b. Lead
    c. Polishing

3.6 Ceramic

5.1 Incinerators

    a. Containers
    b. General waste
    c. Sewage sludge
    d. Clinical waste
    e. Crematoria
    f. Animal crematoria

5.2 Solvent & oil recovery

6.2 Di-isocyanates

6.5 Coating

    a. Metal containers
    b. Respraying
    c. Vehicles
    d. Appliances & others
    e. Fabric
    f. Printing
    g. Coil

  h. Adhesive
  i. Paper
  j. Film
  k. Powder

6.6 Coating manufacture

  a. Ink
  b. Paint
  c. Adhesive
  d. Powder and resin
  e. Metal powders

6.7 Timber

  a. Manufacture
  b. Chemical treatment
  c. Chipboard

6.8 Animal and plant treatment

  a. Animal rendering
  b. Fish meal & fish oil
  c. Maggot breeding
  d. Skins & hides
  e. By-product dealers
  f. Animal feed
  g. Edible sausage casings
  h. Pet food
  i. Fur breeding
  j. Composing fertiliser manufacture
  k. Other edible by-product

NB This is a general list and readers are advised to examine in detail the full definitions of prescribed processes.

APPENDIX C

The Meaning of BATNEEC*

BATNEEC (or formulations which are equivalent in meaning) is gaining increasing currency in international standards relating to environmental protection. The most notable documents are the EC Air Framework Directive (84/360) and the EC Dangerous Substances Directive (76/464) and their daughters. The EC Directives use the term 'best available technology'. The Environmental Protection Act uses the term 'best available technique'. 'Techniques' are intended to include technology, but in addition to hardware are intended to include operational factors.

All processes prescribed under Pt I of the Environmental Protection Act are subject to the BATNEEC requirements. In general terms what is BATNEEC for one process is likely to be BATNEEC for a comparable process. But in each case it is in practice for the enforcing authority (subject to appeal to the Secretary of State) to decide what is BATNEEC for the individual process and it will take into account variable factors such as configuration, size and other individual characteristics of the process in doing so. In the last resort the courts could overturn a decision if it was manifestly unreasonably. For reasons discussed later in this paper it will in practice be necessary to have a general working definition of BATNEEC for the guidance of inspectors in the field, of the operators of scheduled processes and of the Secretary of State in determining appeals or in issuing directions to the Chief Inspector and to local authorities.

It should always be borne in mind that BATNEEC is one feature of a complex of objectives set out in s7 of the Act which has to be achieved in determining an application. In deciding an application no release can be tolerated which constitutes a recognised health hazard, either in the short term or long term.

In reducing the emissions to the lowest practicable amount, account needs to be taken of local conditions and circumstances, both of the process and the environment, the current state of knowledge and the financial implications in relation to capital expenditure and revenue cost.

---

* Best Available Techniques Not Entailing Excessive Cost.

BAT

It is necessary to construe the words Best Available Techniques separately and together.

'Techniques' embraces both the process used and how that process is operated. The word should be taken to mean the concept and design of the process, the components of which it is made up and the manner in which they are connected together to make the whole. It should also be taken to include matters such as staff numbers, working methods, training, supervision and manner of operating the process.

'Available' should be taken to mean procurable by any operator of the class of process in question. It does not imply that the technology is in general use, but it does require general accessibility. It does not imply that sources outside the UK are 'unavailable'. Nor does it not imply a multiplicity of sources. If there is a monopoly supplier the technique counts as being available provided that any and all operators can procure it.

'Best' must be taken to mean most effective in preventing, minimising or rendering harmless polluting emissions. On this definition, there may be more than one set of techniques that achieves the same degree of effectiveness – ie there may be more than one 'best' techniques. It implies that the technology effectiveness has been demonstrated.

NEEC

'Not entailing excessive cost' needs to be taken in two contexts, depending on whether it is applied to new processes or to existing processes.

The presumption will be that best available techniques will be used, but that presumption can be modified by economic considerations where it can be shown that the costs of applying Best Available Techniques would be excessive in relation to the environmental protection to be achieved. If, for instance there is one technology which reduces the emission of a polluting substance by 90 per cent and another which reduces the emissions by 95 per cent but at four times the cost, it may be a proper judgment to hold that because of the small benefit and the great cost the second technology would entail excessive cost. If the emissions were particularly dangerous, on the other hand, it may be proper to judge that the additional cost was not excessive.

Existing processes

In applying NEEC to BAT for existing processes we are essentially concerned with the timing of the upgrading of old processes to new standards. We are guided to some extent by Articles 12 and 13 of the Air Framework Directive.

Article 13, which applies to processes existing prior to 1987 requires certain factors to be taken into account.

'In the light of an examination of developments as regards the best available technology and the environmental situation, the Member States shall implement policies and strategies, including appropriate

measures, for the gradual adaptation of existing plants belonging to the categories given in Annex 1 to the best available technology, taking into account in particular:
- the plant's technical characteristics,
- its rate of utilisation and length of its remaining life,
- the nature and volume of polluting emissions from it,
- the desirability of not entailing excessive costs for the plant concerned, having regard in particular to the economic situation of undertakings belonging to the category in question.'

Article 12, which is concerned with keeping authorisations for existing processes up to date with respect to technological developments, sets out somewhat less extensive guidelines.

Emission standards

Clearly BATNEEC may be expressed in technological terms – ie a requirement to employ specified hardware. But given the definition of 'Best' above, it may also be expressed in terms of emission standards. Having identified the best technology and the emission values it is capable of producing, it would be possible to express BATNEEC as a performance standard ie that technology which produces emission standards of X or better, where X are the values yielded by the identified BATNEEC. BATNEEC should normally be expressed in these terms in order to avoid the risk of constraining the development of cleaner technology or of restricting operators' choice of means to achieve a given standard.

The promulgation of BATNEEC

In each individual case the Chief Inspector or the local authority must decide what is BATNEEC and translate it into requirements in the conditions of the authorisation. There must, however, be consistency across the board. Individual inspectors should not be required to re-invent the wheel each time they determine an application for an authorisation. Process operators, and indeed the public, will require an assurance that BATNEEC is being applied in a rational and consistent way. That dictates that the process of arriving at BATNEEC must be open and explicit. It is proposed to convey this information through the medium of published guidance to HMIP inspectors and to local authorities on the application of integrated pollution regulation or air pollution control (including BATNEEC factors) for classes of process. Where guidance is issued by the Secretary of State it must be taken into account by the enforcing authority in determining an application.

Openness

IPC is an open and explicit system of control. Guidance will give due consideration to the opinions of those who are being regulated and will be subject to consultation with the public as represented by interested bodies. It follows that guidance relating to the specification of BATNEEC and the timetable of application to existing processes will be preceded by consultation with representatives of the operators of the category of processes involved and, at a suitable point in time, the public more generally. The coverage of the guidance should be comprehensive, and subject to some form of publicly available programme. This is particularly relevant to the orderly implementation of Pt 1 of the Environmental Protection Act. Process operators will have notice of the order and timescale in which they will be brought into the system and be provided with the rationale for the priorities set.

APPENDIX D

APPLICATION FOR AUTHORISATION UNDER IPC

HER MAJESTY'S INSPECTORATE OF POLLUTION

The Environmental Protection Act 1990, Section 6(3)

1. Applicant's Details

Application No.

Registered Name and
Address of Applicant:

Post Code:

Companies House Registration Number

Address of Process Location:
[if mobile process then
 principal place of business]

Post Code:
National Grid Reference:

Address to which
invoices should be sent:

Post Code:

Payment Method: Cheque/Direct Debit/Payable Order/Other (please
specify) . . . .
Payment by credit card not acceptable

Amount attached to application:

Local District Council area in which
premises are located:

(if mobile process then local district council of principal place of business)

Waste Regulation Authority area:

Sewerage Undertakers:

Are there any plans to discharge to
controlled waters?   Yes/No

Are there any details you consider need to be covered by commercial
confidentiality?   If YES then please see the attached guidance note
which details the procedures you must follow.

*Please enclose copies of any consents/agreements/authorisations, etc that are
currently held in respect to releases of substances from this process to the
environment.*

Please list below any copies or additional information enclosed with
this application form:

Is this an application for a mobile   Y/N
process?

2. Applicant's Declaration

I hereby declare that all information contained in this application is, to the best of my knowledge, correct.

Signed

Date

note: it is an offence under section 23(h) of the Act to provide false or misleading information

Schedule reference number:

Components contained within process (see guidance note):

Total Number of Components:

Section 2   Process information

1. State the category and purpose of the process.

2. Identify the prescribed substances involved in the process and any other substances which might cause harm if released into any environmental medium.

3. Describe briefly the process and the techniques that will ensure that the pollution potential of the process is minimised including the process controls and the handling and storage of process materials.

4. Describe the pollution abatement plant that will be used for reducing the release of prescribed substances to a minimum and rendering harmless any other substances which might cause harm.

5. What redundancy is available to cope with the breakdown or planned maintenance of plant?

6. Describe how the abatement plant copes with the full range of operating circumstances of the plant.

7. State whether the process will be operated continuously and give details of the staff employed to control the process.

8. Does this proposal constitute a commitment to the use of 'Best Available Techniques' (BAT)? Answer Yes or No.

If No, set out the argument in support of the case that alternative techniques would entail excessive costs.

9. Give appropriate details if this application takes into account any plans, directions or prescriptions by the Secretary of State.

Section 3   Releases

1. Detail the release points and quantities of substances set out in section 2.2 above for which authorisation is sought during the operation of the process
   (i) to the air
   (ii) to the water.

2. What is the consequence of the release of these substances taking into account local circumstances? Give references for any assessment factors used.

3. Describe the other wastes which will be generated and state for which wastes an off site treatment or disposal route will be sought and whether it has been secured. Is the pollution which may be caused to the environment from the permitted disposal of such wastes sensitive to any of the factors associated with the process on the site? What is the requirement to store such wastes on site prior to disposal?

4. Summarise briefly how the design and operation of this process will achieve the requirement to 'minimise the pollution to the environment taken as a whole by the releases having regard to the best practicable environmental option available as respects the substances which may be released'.

5. What research if any is being carried out or sponsored by the company in the context of BAT to further reduce the creation of wastes limit the release of polluting substances and assess the impact of those that are released?

Section 4   Compliance

The applicant will be required as a condition of authorisation to make and implement adequate arrangements to demonstrate compliance with the conditions of the authorisation. This section is for the Company to propose how it could demonstrate compliance with possible authorisation conditions on

    (i) feedstocks
   (ii) process parameters
  (iii) performance of pollution abatement plant
  (iv) emission monitoring or sampling
   (v) environmental sampling
  (vi) analytical procedures
 (vii) quality assurance plans
(viii) record keeping

Reference should be made to British Standards Institute and other accepted procedures wherever possible.

If there is insufficient space on the application form then please continue on separate sheets.

2. CERTIFICATE OF AUTHORISATION

HER MAJESTY'S INSPECTORATE OF POLLUTION

Environmental Protection Act 1990

ERNEST NONESUCH, CERTIFICATE OF AUTHORISATION

Ref No

The Chief Inspector, Her Majesty's Inspectorate of Pollution in accordance with section—of the [Act] has determined the application dated——[and further information date——] from

Ernest Nonesuch plc

Registerd office—— No——

and authorises this Company to carry on the process(es) as detailed in the application being a process(es) prescribed in Part A of Regulations made under [Section 2(1) of the Act] namely

at the premises occupied by the Company at——within the District of——in the County of——subject to the process controls and release limits set out in the schedule and the further conditions and limitations set out in pages—— attached.

Signed...............................

A person authorised to sign on behalf of the Chief Inspector

Dated the.................................

Schedule

1. Process controls [eg]

Parameters	Restriction
Temperature	$1110°C \pm 25°C$
Throughout	> 25 tonnes/hr
Feedstocks	>1 ppm Codmium

2. Releases to air

Releases of substances by specified outlets (OS ref.................)

nominated stock   substance   max concentration   max per [day]

3. Releases of prescribed substances to surface waters

nominated off site routes eg outfall, sewer, etc (OS ref...............)

4. Transfer of wastes containing prescribed substances other than for deposit including

(i) exclamation
(ii) waste treatment (liquid)
(iii) waste conditioning

1. Process plants

The Company shall only carry out the authorised processes in those process units and plants and in those parts of the site detailed in the applications. Without prejudice to the general condition in [section 7(4) of the Act] the process shall be carried out so that the generation of waste [and the release of substances] are minimised and so that the parameters detailed in the schedule are complied with. In addition the Company shall [ensure that   ].

2. Containment of substances

The Company shall make and implement appropriate arrangements to ensure that raw materials, process intermediates, products and wastes are contained as described in the application and that any releases are only via nominated routes detailed in the schedule. In addition the Company shall:

[spray/cover stocks of raw materials etc]
[precautions during transfer]

3. Treatment and release of gaseous substances

The Company shall make and implement adequate arrangements to collect and treat [process gases] [gases mists and dusts] and ensure that it shall not release any substances to air except by those means detailed in the application and in accordance with the limits detailed in the schedule. In addition the Company shall [ensure that emissions shall be colourless and free from droplets].

4. Treatment and release of liquid substances

The Company shall make and implement adequate arrangements to collect and treat liquid process arisings as described in the application and that it shall not discharge any treated effluent except by those routes and in accordance with the limits detailed in the schedule. In addition the Company shall: [ensure that ....].

5. Conditioning of process wastes

The Company shall make and implement adequate arrangements to condition [process] [incinerate] wastes as described in the application. In addition the Company shall [ensure that ....].

6. Demonstration of compliance

[Before commencement of the process the Company shall make available to any nominated Inspector copies of the arrangements required by this author- isation.] [The Company shall prepare a document to the satisfaction of the

Chief Inspector specifying the means employed to ensure compliance with this authorisation. Thereafter the Company shall obtain his written approval before making any changes to the means as specified in the document.]

(1) Sampling and testing

The Company shall:

(a) take and analyse such samples of substances which may be released as are necessary for the purpose of this authorisation;
(b) take and analyse such samples of substances which may be released and conduct other tests and surveys as the Chief Inspector may from time to time require;
(c) make and keep a record of such analysis test or survey;
(d) retain or despatch samples of substances which may be released as directed by the Chief Inspector.

(2) Records and provision of information

The Company shall:

(a) make and keep a record of such process parameters as may be necessary to demonstrate compliance with this authorisation and in a manner approved by the Chief Inspector in writing;
(b) make and keep a record of substances released as may be necessary to demonstrate compliance with this authorisation and in a manner approved by the Chief Inspector in writing;
(c) keep the records required to be made in a manner and for a period and in a place approved by the Chief Inspector in writing, and ensure that any amendment to the records leaves the original entry clear and legible.

7. Special conditions relating to limits or plans set by the Secretary of State

8. Provision of information for the public register

[Is this required as an authorisation Condition?]

9. Interpretation etc

10. *Subject to the condition in section 6 above this authorisation shall come into effect on* ....

APPENDIX E

A NOTE ON THE INFLUENCE OF EUROPEAN COMMUNITY LEGISLATION

Introduction

There is a strong impetus in the pace of legislation flowing from the environment programme of the European Community. It must be concluded that this is inevitably having a profound effect upon the Government's parliamentary programme and the consequences for business and industry in the UK. The two major statutes dealing with environment standards, the Water Act 1989 and the Environmental Protection Act 1990 accommodate and, to a certain extent, anticipate what has emerged and will develop from Brussels during the 1990s. The government's environment white paper 'This Common Inheritance' deals comprehensively with what it perceives are its responsibilities within the context of Europe. Paragraph 3.8 sets out the approach:

> 'The Government therefore believes that the Community's programme for the environment must be vigorous and forward-looking, tackling issues in ways which are consistent with the responsibilities we owe to future generations and which encourage people to use Europe's natural resources in sustainable ways. The polluter must pay wherever possible. Action must be based on the best science available, but scientific uncertainty must not be an excuse for delay where there are clear threats of damage that could be serious or irreversible. As in Britain, we must weigh the costs of proposals for action carefully against the benefits and try to make sure that priority is given to measures that give the best and most urgent results most cost-effectively. It is the Government's aim to make sure that the standards that the Community sets do their job effectively, and that they do not put British people and firms at an unfair disadvantage; and to see that all EC policies – not just those on the environment itself – take environmental questions properly into account.'

The basis of the Common Market environment programme

The legislation programme of the European Community is in the form mainly of directives and regulations. The basis of environmental directives and

112

regulations is (since 1st July 1987) article 130R of the revised Treaty of Rome, brought into force so far as the UK is concerned by the Single European Act 1986. Article 130R2 requires that 'action by the Community relating to the environment shall be based on the principles that preventative action should be taken, that environmental damage should, as a priority, be rectified at source, and that the polluter should pay. The article also acknowledges the far reaching and all pervading influence of environmental protection in that it requires that protection to be a component of the Community's other policies'. This has been echoed by UK government in the white paper.

The distinction between directives and regulations is often not understood fully. Directives are in effect an instruction to member states to achieve the objectives of the directive in question. How they do this is a matter for individual states although achievement is usually by legislation or other codes. Partly because of slow progress by certain member states in implementing directives, there now is some emphasis on the power of the regulation. Once confirmed, regulations passed by the Community directly bind individuals and organisations within each member state. This means that no further legislation is required within member states although this frequently follows as a matter of consistency and clarification. Enforcement remains the responsibility of the member state, although overall policing of the performance rests with the Community and, increasingly in the future, by the European Environment Agency (EEA).

Established by council regulation 1210/90, the EEA's present role is the assembly (through national agencies) of information. This is of course a restricted role and one which has drawn some criticism from environmental organisations throughout Europe. It is certainly a very tentative start and is no doubt a reflection of hesitancy on the part of member state's governments about re-assigning enforcement responsibilities (and thereby political influence thereon) to what would be a much more independent body. A better argument for the UK and some of the other member states is that each already has in place a very well-developed regime of regulation and duplication of this would be highly undesirable. The role of the EEA is due to be reviewed after two years and it seems inevitable that members of the Commission will see a stronger range of duties being devolved, including the monitoring of the implementation of Community environmental legislation.

Directives already approved by the EC

Figure 1 lists some of the more significant directives and regulations concerning environmental matters (see page 116).

New European initiatives

(a) *Amendment of the Waste Directive 75/442/EEC.* The amended directive, published in 1988, is now approved. Its scope includes a stricter definition of waste, a greater emphasis on the encouragement of recycling, the strengthening of controls on disposal sites, injunction to member states to become self-sufficient in waste disposal capacity, to contribute towards an

integrated network of disposal installations and to require registration of
waste carriers and brokers.

(b) *Hazardous Waste.* This revised directive is reported to have been agreed
by environment ministers, with formal adoption in 1991. It will amend
the directive on toxic and dangerous waste 78/319/EEC. The function of
this document is to define hazardous waste in more detail, strengthen
controls, extending them to producers, including the control of collection, transport and temporary storage and requiring hazardous waste
disposal plans.

(c) *Landfill Directive.* This document has been the subject of hard negotia-
tion. It seeks to identify three types of landfill, a) hazardous waste, b)
municipal and non-hazardous waste, c) inert waste. Originally it sought
to exclude certain wastes including clinical or liquids. Some member
states, including the UK, have not been happy with the definitions and it
is noticeable tht the sixth draft has now lifted the ban on liquids, provided
they are compatible with the type of wastes acceptable in each individual
landfill and with the operating procedure at the site. Co-disposal of
hazardous wastes, previously not permitted by the draft, has also been
accommodated.

The directive will also require that landfill is specifically to be rejected
in ground water protection zones, nature protection zones, areas of high
risk of floods, subsidence or inadequate hydro-geological conditions.
There were a number of specific locational requirements including
minimum distances between the landfill and sensitive areas and resources
eg residences, water bodies etc. It is noticeable that in the later drafts the
specific minimum separation distances have been dropped in favour of a
more general, pragmatic approach, but with landfilling standards in
harmony from state to state. Landfill operators would be obliged to
provide financial guarantees in respect of environmental liabilities and
aftercare. Environmental assessments will be required for all sites except
those dealing with inert wastes. Finally, the 'polluter pays' principle is
manifested in requirements that landfill charges must cover all operational costs and that a state waste management fund (no doubt with
industry contribution) should be established to deal with damage from all
waste disposal which is incapable of being dealt with by other means eg
through the licensing system.

(d) *Civil liability for waste.* Of great importance to landfill operators would be
this proposed directive which would impose on the producer of waste
liability under civil law for damage and injury to the environment caused
by waste, irrespective of fault on his part. Even the existence of a site
licence will not protect him. A 'producer' has the ordinary meaning of
that word but is widely defined to include an importer, the person
responsible for transit and the operator of the landfill site. So widely has
the definition been drawn that it is felt that it could extend liability to
others responsible. This might even include a mortgagee or receiver.
Proceedings could be taken to prevent any further deposit or pollution,
for the costs of preventive measures, damages for injury to person or
peroperty, costs of restoration. Class actions would be permitted. De-

fences would be very limited, to *force majeure* (in certain circumstances), contributory negligence and act of a third party. There would be a long limitation period which would run for three years from the time that the plaintiff became aware or should have become aware of the damage, with a final limitation of 30 years after the damage or injury occurred. Bearing in mind that such damage or injury might arise a considerable number of years after the operation has closed, such limitation period might be approaching one hundred years. Whilst the House of Lords Select Committee has generally endorsed the principles, the draft has run into a lot of opposition from certain member states, as a result of which its progress is likely to be considerably slowed.

(e) Environmental auditing. Also on the distant horizon are the European Commission's plans for an environmental auditing directive. A draft proposal was published in 1991 but is only at the 'thinking aloud' stage at the present time. A best guess is that a directive might be approved in the mid-1990s. Of over 50 industrial activities which would be proposed to be subject to self-assessment, there are included installations for the incineration or disposal of domestic wastes and for the disposal of dangerous or toxic waste. Depending on the precise definition of 'installations' it seems more than possible that landfill operations will be caught. The draft proposes a voluntary code (i) to carry out a periodic self-assessment of environmental performance (ii) that in certain circumstances external verification would be provided by independent registered auditors, and (iii) that the audit in some form should be reported to the public.

(f) Recycling. The approach to recycling by the Commission has been largely on the basis of an attack on individual product areas. The first of these was in relation to 'beverage containers' (85/339/EEC) which required member states to establish recycling programmes, although these could be voluntary. However, there is a new proposal which may well set minimum recycling targets.

(g) Batteries containing mercury, lead or cadmium are the subject of a recently agreed directive. Recyclability will be the subject of compulsory labelling and an excess of mercury in batteries will be banned as from the beginning of 1993.

(h) In capital expenditure terms, the most significant of 1991's crop of directives is that dealing with standards and requirements for supply and treatment of municipal waste water (sewage). Estimates of the likely UK cost exceed £1.5 billion. This may well have to be spent in 10 years if the ambitious programme is to be met. It is to be borne in mind that simply the borrowing cost of this level of expenditure will exceed the current turnover of some water companies. The implications of the huge figures call into question the regular absence of any cost-benefit analysis of EC proposals. Tax and charge-payers in the UK may complain but the costs to Mediterranean States will be much greater. A reminder of the influence of Brussels could hardly be more stark.

EEC Legislation

Waste on land

1975 Council Directive on the Disposal of Waste Oils (75/439/EEC)
1975 Council Directive on Waste (75/442/EEC)
1976 Council Directive on the Disposal of PCBs (76/403/EEC)
1978 Council Directive on Toxic and Dangerous Waste (78/319/EEC)
1984 Council Directive on the Supervision and Control within the European Community of the Transfrontier Shipment of Hazardous Waste (84/631/EEC)
1986 Council Directive on the Protection of the Environment when Sewage Sludge is Used in Agriculture (86/278/EEC)
1991 Council Directive on Waste (91/156/EEC) replaces most of 75/442/EEC.

Pollution of inland waters

1973 Council Directive on Detergents (73/404/EEC)
1973 Council Directive on the Control of the Biodegradability of Anionic Surfactants (73/405/EEC)
1975 Council Directive on the Quality of Bathing Water (76/160/EEC)
1976 Council Directive on Pollution caused by the Discharge of Certain Dangerous Substances into the Aquatic Environment (76/464/EEC)
1978 Council Directive on the Quality of Fresh Waters needed to Support Fish Life (78/659/EEC)
1979 Council Directive on the Quality required of Shellfish Waters (79/923/EEC)
1979 Council Directive on the Protection of Groundwater against Pollution caused by Certain Dangerous Substances (80/68/EEC)
1980 Council Directive on the Quality of Water for Human Consumption (80/778/EEC)
1989 Council Directive on Pollution by Waste from the Titanium Dioxide Industry (89/428/EEC)
1991 Council Directive on Urban Waste Water Treatment (91/271/EEC)

Atmospheric pollution

1970 Council Directive on Air Pollution by Motor Vehicles (70/220/EEC)
1975 Council Directive on the Sulphur Content of Certain Liquid Fuels (75/716/EEC)
1977 Council Directive on the Emission of Pollutants by Diesel Engines for Use in Tractors (77/537/EEC)
1980 Council Directive on Air Quality Limit Values for Sulphur Dioxide and Suspended Particulates (80/779/EEC)
1982 Council Directive on a Limit Value for Lead in the Air (82/884/EEC)

1984 Council Directive on the Combating of Air Pollution from Industrial Plants (84/360/EEC)
1985 Council Directive on Air Quality Standards for Nitrogen Dioxide (85/203/EEC)
1985 Council Directive on the Lead Content of Petrol (85/210/EEC)
1987 Council Directive on Measures to be Taken against the Emission of Gaseous Pollutants from Diesel Engines for Use in Vehicles (88/77/EEC)
1988 Council Regulation (EEC) No 3322 on Certain Chlorofluorocarbons and Halons which Deplete the Ozone Layer
1988 Council Directive on the Limitation of Emissions of Certain Pollutants into the Air from Large Combustion Plants (88/609/EEC)
1989 Council Directive on the Prevention of Air Pollution from New Municipal Waste Incineration Plants (89/369/EEC)
1989 Council Directive on the Reduction of Air Pollution from Existing Municipal Waste-Incineration Plants (89/429/EEC)
1991 Council Regulation of Substances that Deplete the Ozone Layer (91/594/EEC)

Pollution by noise

1970 Council Directive on Noise from Motor Vehicles (70/157/EEC)
1978 Council Directive on Noise from Motorcycles (78/1015/EEC)
1978 Council Directive on Noise from Construction Plant and Equipment (79/113/EEC)
1979 Council Directive on Noise from Subsonic Aircraft (80/51/EEC)

Dangerous substances or activities

1978 Council Directive prohibiting the Placing on the Market and Use of Plant Protection Products containing Certain Active Substances (79/117/EEC)
1980 Council Directive amending the Directives laying down the Basic Safety Standards for the Health Protection of the General Public and Workers against the Dangers of Ionising Radiation (80/836/EURATOM)
1982 Council Directive on the Major Accident Hazards of Certain Industrial Activities (82/501/EEC)
1987 Council Regulation (Euratom) No 3954/87 laying down Maximum Permitted Levels of Radioactive Contamination of Foodstuffs and of Feedingstuffs following a Nuclear Accident or Any Other Case of Radiological Emergency
1988 Council Regulation (EEC) No 1734/88 Concerning Export from and Import into the Community of Certain Dangerous Chemicals
1990 Commission Regulation (Euratom) No 770/90 laying down Maximum Permitted Levels of Radioactive Contamination of Feeding Stuffs following a Nuclear Accident or Any Other Case of Radiological Emergency

1990 Council Directive on the Contained Use of Genetically Modified Micro-Organisms (90/219/EEC)
1990 Council Directive on the Deliberate Release into the Environment of Genetically Modified Organisms (90/220/EEC)

Environmental impact assessment

1985 Council Directive on the Assessment of the Effects of Certain Public and Private Projects on the Environment (85/337/EEC)

APPENDIX F

FURTHER READING

Control of Pollution Encyclopedia, edited Garner & Harris, published by Bartholomews (two volumes).

Encyclopedia of Environmental Health and Law and Practice, edited Cross, published by Sweet & Maxwell (three volumes).

Halsbury's Laws of England, fourth edition, published by Butterworths.

The Law of the National Rivers Authority, Howarth, published by the National Rivers Authority and Centre for Law in Rural Areas.

Water Pollution Law, W Howarth, published by Shaw & Sons.

Water and Drainage Law, John H Bates, published by Sweet & Maxwell.

EEC Environmental Policy and Britain, Nigel Haigh, second revised edition published by Longman.

Clerk and Lindsell on Tort, published by Sweet & Maxwell.

Index

Praise for **The Elements of Journalism**

"At a time when technological and financial forces are creating formidable challenges to journalism's traditional values, Kovach and Rosenstiel have written an immensely valuable primer on who we are, what we do, and how we should do it."
—David Halberstam

"*The Elements of Journalism* is a remarkable book that does a superb job of describing the problems, articulating the values, outlining the risks, and offering understandable and practical ways to respond to the difficulties of the present state of journalism. *The Elements of Journalism* ought to become required reading for every institution (and individual) engaged in journalism."
—Neil Rudenstine,
President, Harvard University

"Of the many books that have been written about reporting the news, this one best captures the shortcomings, subtleties, and possibilities of modern journalism. It deserves to become as indispensable to journalists and journalism students as *The Elements of Style.*"
—Tom Goldstein,
Dean, Graduate School of Journalism, Columbia University

"Bill Kovach and Tom Rosenstiel . . . have managed to write a brief book with valuable fresh lessons for news disseminators and news consumers. . . . A wonder of this book is how Kovach and Rosenstiel use those abstractions as jumping-off points for fascinating chapters, each filled with compelling examples of exemplary and less-than-exemplary journalistic practice."
—Steve Weinberg,
Christian Science Monitor

"[The] Book of the Century . . . a textbook for everyone involved in Journalism 2001. It is also a monumental job of reporting."
—William German,
San Francisco Chronicle

"In an age when partisan rancor and ratings-driven showmanship have crowded out the more subtle virtues of solid journalism, Tom Rosenstiel and Bill Kovach provide a timely refresher course in the importance of press fundamentals. They remind us that at its best, journalism is a high public calling, and all those who practice it have a deeper obligation to their readers and viewers than to the demands of the market."

—**David Talbot**,
Editor in Chief, Salon.com

"*The Elements of Journalism* is the most important book on the relationship of journalism and democracy published in the last fifty years. Reporters and editors should memorize its standards. Publishers and owners should read it and then take a good look in the mirror. It is rare, indeed, that a text about ideas appears at just the right moment, with the urgency of an intellectual scoop. But what Rosenstiel and Kovach have given us is a map for conversation, debate, and action as we explore the territory of journalism and business values."

—**Roy Peter Clark**,
The Poynter Institute

"This is one of the most provocative books about the role of information in society in more than a generation and one of the most important ever written about the news." —*African Sun Times*

"[A] thoughtful and significant book."

—**Margaret Sullivan**,
Buffalo News

"Incisive, controversial and well presented . . . Kovach and Rosenstiel have issued a clarion call to their colleagues, and they hope that all journalists, editors, and owners of news organizations will incorporate the principles of the profession as they've outlined them into their everyday work." —*Publishers Weekly*